TAKING BACK LENT

MOVING WITH REPENTANCE AND REFLECTION TO THE RESURRECTION

NANCY GOLDEN

Quote by Joseph Fredrickson used with his permission.
Quote by Barbara White used with her permission, Conciliar Post, *Repentance
and Resurrection*, April 23, 2021.

All Scripture quotations, unless otherwise indicated, are taken from the Holy
Bible, New International Version®, NIV®. Copyright ©1973, 1978, 1984, 2011 by
Biblica, Inc.™ Used by permission of Zondervan. All rights reserved
worldwide. www.zondervan.com The "NIV" and "New International Version"
are trademarks registered in the United States Patent and Trademark Office by
Biblica, Inc.™

"Forgive Others" © 2024 by Jane Vaughan
"Love One Another" © 2024 by Phil Golden
"Rescuer and Savior" © 2024 by Kathleen Baldwin
"Daffodils" © 2024 by D. Bailey Wynne
"Joy" © 2024 by David Joshua Golden
"The Colors of Lent" © 2024 by Laura Fritz
All devotionals reprinted by permission of the authors.

For information or inquiries, contact Nancy Golden at
nancy@goldencrossranch.com

Library of Congress Control Number: 2024900750

Published by Golden Cross Ranch LLC
Carrollton, Texas U.S.A.

Cover Photo by Pronoia / Adobe Stock License

Cover Design by Golden Cross Ranch LLC

For Pastor Chad and Pastor Jennifer Burton, who continue to fight the good fight and forward the Gospel every day, eternally impacting the lives around them. Thank you for giving to the Lord.

In loving memory of the great cloud of witnesses that helped shape our lives and are now cheering us on: My parents, Ralph and Leah Venetucci, and my parents-in-law, Bill and Mary Kay Golden.

FOREWORD

One of the best things about being an author is that we can empower each other as we all grow in our craft. We are meant to be in community and the opportunity to invite other authors into this space is one I couldn't pass up.

While I have written the majority of the devotionals found in these pages, you will notice additional authors in Taking Back Lent. Each person is dear to me. They have encouraged me on my own journey and I am honored they have agreed to contribute. While I have written forty-two of the devotionals, you will see theirs sprinkled in.

I am excited for you to hear their different voices. May you be blessed and God glorified by our collective efforts!

INTRODUCTION

Repentance and hope should not be considered opposites. Rather, they are very much the same. The Old Testament uses the Hebrew word לשוב (lashuv) for the word repentance. This quite literally means "to return" or "turn back to" in the same sense as used in directional course correction. Repentance, by its very nature, should bring hope to a person's soul. They are re-aligning themselves back with God!
   —Joseph Fredrickson

We live at the intersection of sin and grace. Repentance for sins is part of the struggle of being a Christian. During Lent we recognize the depth of our sin, our desperate need for a Savior, and the greatness of His mercy. We are preparing our hearts for what is coming, the passion of Christ, His death, and His Resurrection.

This Lenten devotional may be the perfect way to help us reflect on what we can do to lead holy lives while bringing hope to our days. In these pages you will find an easy-to-understand book that is intentionally not very long, so you can savor each reading in a short period of time. You will find it very convenient to fit this devotional into even the busiest of schedules, yet it will help you experience the peace and hope that this special season brings. The daily readings and activities will help you realize God's mercy and graciousness are awaiting you.

We cannot help but see the linking of repentance with the Resurrection. Barbara White in her article "Repentance and Resurrection" in the Conciliar Post states it well:

> Repentance and Resurrection are two acts of the same great divine drama. Jesus himself hints that the two go together: "The time is fulfilled, and the kingdom of God has come near; repent, and believe in the good news" (Mark 1:15). If "Alleluia! The Lord is risen!" is the best good news, then repentance is not merely some inconvenient roadblock on the way to Resurrection, but part of what it means to be an Easter people.

The Resurrection of Jesus is at the heart of the Gospel message, and repentance helps us to get there. We do this by starting each day with a brief devotional that gives us an opportunity to move with repentance and reflection toward the Resurrection:

> Let us throw off everything that hinders and the sin that so easily entangles. And let us run with perseverance the race marked out for us, fixing our eyes on Jesus, the pioneer and perfecter of faith.
> Hebrews12:1b-2a

Lent is observed for forty days, which does not include Sundays, and begins on Ash Wednesday of each year. I did not want to leave you without a daily devotional during the Lenten season, so I have invited five guest authors to write a devotional for five of those Sundays. You will see the author's name attributed to their devotional on those days, along with a delightful interpretation of the colors of Lent in the back of the book. I finish with devotionals for Palm Sunday and Easter Sunday, so you will be able to enjoy a daily devotional beginning on Ash Wednesday and going all the way through the Resurrection.

As you prepare for your Lenten journey, pray for what the Holy Spirit is calling you to do. Just as He led Jesus in the wilderness for forty days, so He will lead you through this season. Many traditions call for emulating Jesus's wilderness journey by fasting. Perhaps you will feel led to fast from food or something else, as an expression of your dependence on God's grace. Or perhaps you will feel led to do something rather than to do without something, to reflect God's love to others. Whatever you choose is between you and the Lord - He knows your heart.

As you move toward Easter, experience His transforming love for you and become more conformed to the image of Christ. Repent, reflect, and share in His Resurrection! I pray this devotional blesses you and enables you to take back Lent as you move through this special season of renewing your faith.

May His Grace and Peace be with you always.

ASH WEDNESDAY - DAY ONE

NANCY GOLDEN

A sh Wednesday traditionally marks the beginning of the first day of Lent, an important event in the Christian liturgical calendar. Lent is a time of solemn self-reflection and confession that parallels what Jesus experienced during His 40 days in the wilderness. While we will be exploring and reflecting on the meaning of that wilderness journey and applying it in our own lives, today, our focus will be on Ash Wednesday (also referred to as the Day of Ashes).

You may have participated in Lent as part of your church or denomination tradition, or you may have, at some point in the past, been startled and wondered why you see people walking around with a black-colored cross smudged across their foreheads. You may have deduced that it has a religious meaning associated with the Christian faith, and in fact, you would be correct. So, let's take today to understand the significance of this special and solemn day in the Christian faith.

Interestingly enough, preparation for Ash Wednesday begins almost a year prior. Palm Sunday is another important holiday in the Christian church, which commemorates Jesus's final entrance into Jerusalem (Mark 11:1-11). His followers greeted

Him in grand style as the coming king, and people waved palm branches in homage to Him. In many church traditions, church leaders hand out palm branches on Palm Sunday, and the congregation replicates the scene from Scripture during the worship service. The palm branches are then gathered and burned, and the ashes are set aside for use on Ash Wednesday the following year. The priest or pastor then mixes this substance with oil to make the sign of the cross.

Depending on a person's church tradition, the imparting of this symbol can occur in one of a variety of ways. Often, they attend a mass or church service, and it is a time of both personal and communal repentance. A message centering around Genesis 3:19 is frequently given, and afterward, the congregation is invited to come forward to receive their ashes. The priest or pastor will typically say, "Repent and believe in the Gospel," or "Remember that you are dust, and to dust you shall return," as they use their thumb dipped in ashes to draw the cross on the person's forehead.

Whether you are able to participate in the actual receiving of ashes or not, what matters most is what is going on in your own heart. Ash Wednesday is an important reminder of our need for repentance and our mortality, but also that through our repentance and obedience to God comes everlasting life.

TODAY'S ACTIVITY: The story of Ash Wednesday can be found in the following verses. Take a few minutes to meditate on them.

Genesis 2:7 informs us that we were created from dust. God formed man from the dust of the ground, and then His very breath brought us to life!

Genesis 3:19 tells us the consequences of the Fall, when man and woman were cast out of the garden—that we were made from dust and to dust we shall return.

Psalm 51:7-10 is how we should respond—David's cry for repentance is also our own.

REREAD the words of David in Psalm 51, "Create in me a pure heart, O God" (Psalm 51:10), and reflect on those words. Rejoice in the fact that—while we all need to repent—we are not in it alone. David calls out to God for help, and so can we. The Psalms are a great example for us in how to pray. Take a few minutes and pray Psalm 51 to the One who loves you beyond measure.

THURSDAY – DAY TWO

NANCY GOLDEN

Yesterday, we discovered where the ashes used on Ash Wednesday came from. Let's pause a moment to study the significance of this connection. Why use the ashes of the palm branches that paid homage to Christ, to mark the symbol of the cross on a Christian's forehead? Keep in mind that the branches are used to recognize Jesus as the coming king in what is often referred to as the triumphal entry— Jesus riding on the foal of a donkey in fulfillment of Old Testament prophecy. It is on this occasion that Jesus makes His claim public. He is the Messiah and eagerly awaited King of Israel.

Consider this. The branches used to recognize Jesus as the long-awaited King and Messiah are consumed by fire and made into ashes. These same branches have been refined into a substance to mark the forehead of a believer who uses the opportunity to reflect on their need for a Savior. The branches were used to recognize an earthly conquering king. The ashes symbolize humility and anointing of the King, who came not to conquer Rome, but to rule in the kingdom of our hearts.

TODAY'S ACTIVITY: Reflect on Paul's words about Jesus in Philippians 2:6-7,

> Who, being in very nature God, did not consider equality with God something to be used to his own advantage;
> rather, he made himself nothing by taking the very nature of a servant, being made in human likeness.

What example does that set for our own journey? When we get enamored by our own self-importance or feel driven toward earthly measures of success, it's good to remember that the King of the universe made himself nothing. God does not desire our achievements, awards, or trophies. He desires our hearts.

Galatians 5:22-23 tells us, "But the fruit of the Spirit is love, joy, peace, forbearance, kindness, goodness, faithfulness, gentleness, and self-control." Choose one and focus on how you can strive toward achieving it – practice setting goals that have eternal value rather than earthly acclaim.

FRIDAY – DAY THREE

NANCY GOLDEN

Hebrews 12:1-2 is a wonderful Scripture to guide us through the Lenten season:

Therefore, since we are surrounded by such a great cloud of witnesses, let us throw off everything that hinders and the sin that so easily entangles. And let us run with perseverance the race marked out for us, fixing our eyes on Jesus, the pioneer and perfecter of faith. For the joy set before him he endured the cross, scorning its shame, and sat down at the right hand of the throne of God.

Often, when people think about Lent, they mistake the solemnity of the season as a reason for sadness. Reflecting on our sin is not a joyful topic, after all. But a season of fasting, praying, and almsgiving should be a season of joy (one of the fruits of the Spirit) in that we are drawing closer to God through these penitential actions – allowing His grace to flow over us.

Giving up something for Lent is not a punishment for our sins, which would be very bad theology robbing us of the meaning of God's incredible grace – the forgiveness we have through the atoning sacrifice of His Son. Lent is a season to experience God's love for us in great measure while living in the hope of the Resurrection!

By participating in the Lenten practice of giving up something, we come to find we didn't need it after all – that God is all we need. Lent is a wonderful time to grow spiritually stronger, and by releasing what we have been clinging to, we become truly free.

So let us throw off everything that hinders and the sin that so easily entangles and set our eyes on the One that provides everything we could ever need!

TODAY'S ACTIVITY: Reflect on the things in your life that divert your attention away from God and His purposes. Be careful to distinguish between your God-given passions and the temptations of the world. You may be called to temporarily fast from what God has planted in your heart, and that is okay, but don't mistake that for something you should give up permanently. Fast from those things that come from the world, for by doing so, you will find that God fills that void more than you can ever imagine.

My own personal example: I love horses and ride every chance I get. When I ride, it's also a chance for me to connect with God on my horse – I often sing praise and worship songs and pray. But if I started riding without that spiritual component and rode to the point of neglecting others and my responsibilities, it would be wise for me to fast from riding so that I could regain a spiritual balance.

Since that is not the case, I would choose to fast from social media, as I find myself occasionally pulled in and wasting a lot of time on it that could be much better spent. I could commit to reading my Bible during the time I would normally connect on social media, or do something for someone – perhaps writing a card of encouragement to someone that God put on my heart.

We are each unique – spend some time thinking about what you feel called to do for Lent and commit to doing it. There are no right or wrong answers; just think about what would be pleasing to God in your own life.

SATURDAY – DAY FOUR

NANCY GOLDEN

The words of Psalm 8:4 would give the most prideful person pause:

what is mankind that you are mindful of them, human beings that you care for them?

This week, we have spent some time reflecting on our not-so-enviable state—that we are made of dust. Dust really is the great equalizer. Think about it: once we are reduced to dust, we are indistinguishable from other human beings. Presidents, kings and queens, beggars, or thieves all look the same when reduced to dust. But that also brings home the fact that God views each of us through the same lens of love, no matter our station in life.

PSALM 103:13-14 TELLS US,

> As a father has compassion on his children, so the Lord has compassion on those who fear him; for he knows how we are formed, he remembers that we are dust.

It is not what we have accomplished in our life that pleases God—but a humble heart that loves Him and holds Him in awe and reverence because He is God. Fear in this context does not simply mean to be afraid of Him but to regard Him with awe and wonder; respect Him and be obedient to His good and perfect will.

VERSES 15-16 CONTINUE,

> The life of mortals is like grass, they flourish like a flower of the field; the wind blows over it and it is gone, and its place remembers it no more.

That does sound depressing until we realize that Psalm 103 is a study in contrasts—our transient earthly existence contrasted with God's everlasting love for us.

IN VERSES 17-18, we learn,

> But from everlasting to everlasting the Lord's love is with those who fear him, and his righteousness with their children's chil-dren—with those who keep his covenant and remember to obey his precepts.

There are some important things we need to draw from here. We are indeed frail, transient dust mites. It makes me feel like Pigpen from Peanuts. But God has entered into an everlasting covenant with us. Praise God—He is faithful even when we aren't! Let's take that further and cross into the New Testament. God's everlasting love for us is so great that His Son voluntarily died on the cross for us—creatures made of dust. It's hard to fathom that great of a love.

TODAY'S ACTIVITY: Read Psalm 103 and reflect on the entire Psalm. Rejoice in the everlasting love God has for transient creatures made of dust and how He has given us a way out of our earthly predicament through His Son, Jesus Christ.

SUNDAY - GUEST DEVOTIONAL

PASTOR JANE VAUGHAN

In Matthew 18:21-22, Peter asked Jesus, "Lord, if another member of the church sins against me, how often should I forgive? As many as seven times?" Jesus replied, "Not seven times, but, I tell you, seventy-seven times."

We are much like Peter; we want to forgive those who have sinned against us, but we also want to be proud of how much we've forgiven others. Look how very special we think we are! Jesus is telling Peter that counting is irrelevant – just do it.

Forgiving others is challenging. We know God forgives us of our sins when we sincerely ask and repent, but we often have a hard time forgiving others. Think about all the stuff you carry around, the resentments, the self-justifying, the pity. Have you ever considered how all that garbage is weighing you down? You drag it around like a rotting sack of potatoes. Today, let's get rid of it. If the Master of the universe is quick to forgive you, shouldn't you be quick to forgive others as well?

～

TODAY'S ACTIVITY: Try this today and get rid of some of your garbage.

Sit in a quiet place where you can close your eyes, uncross your legs, and concentrate. Think first of a receptacle—my favorite is a trunk with a curved top. After you have chosen your receptacle, put it aside.

Now, spend some time bringing out and lining up your resentments, your anger, those hurts, and arguments with others. Perhaps someone wounded you with their ugly words, or you hurt someone else with your words. Bring it out, line it up, and name each one. Take all the time you need.

Now, get your receptacle and start putting each resentment, each anger, each hurt into the box or trunk or suitcase—whatever you have.

Seal it up, lock it... then the hard part. Ask God to take it from you—ask God to put it completely out of your reach. He will take it from you. Breathe slowly for a few seconds. Now, thank God for taking it and putting it where you can never find it again.

Rejoice that you feel lighter—more joyful. God has taken your garbage, and you are free of it! Jesus frees us from our sins and the sins of others. Thanks be to God!

MONDAY – DAY FIVE

NANCY GOLDEN

L ent reminds us that we are both mortal and in need of forgiveness. It is a time of repentance. I was reflecting on what that might look like. God made us to be in community but being in a relationship can also be very messy. I had a situation happen recently which caused me emotional angst. I was upset at another person's behavior, someone I cared about. I didn't think they were being reasonable. I went so far as to call them out on the behavior, expecting them to show some level of contriteness. Instead, they chose not to acknowledge any responsibility.

While I was very frustrated, I chose not to escalate the situation. What happened just lay there between us. It was evident to me that our friendship would not be repaired unless I initiated it. But I felt like I was the one who was wronged. So, what should I do?

What a great reminder that Jesus was perfect, without sin, yet He chose to bear our sins for us so we could claim His righteousness for our own. If the King of the universe left the heavens to go to the cross for us, how can I be so arrogant as to insist that my offended pride should be salved before our relationship can be restored? Jesus has never said we should be doormats, but we should be humble and not have to always forward our own way. Some of us are more mature and further along on our spiritual walk. Sometimes, we are called not to worry about who was right or wrong, but rather, to do what we need to do to restore the relationship.

So, I reached out to my friend and apologized for what they had perceived as an unjustified attack on their behavior. While they acknowledged that they had been hurt, they never extended any apology to match my own. But you know what? That's okay. Our relationship has been restored.

We don't have to be vindicated, even when we believe we are in the right. If we can love someone with the same unconditional love that Jesus has for us, we come one step closer to becoming more like Him. And I'll take that any day over being proven correct.

TODAY'S ACTIVITY: Take a few minutes to reflect on any relationships you have in your life that need repair. Think about what may be preventing reconciliation with that person. Is there something you can do, an olive branch that you can extend? God loves it when we reconcile with one another.

Reconciliation is challenging (just think of what Jesus did for us so we can be reconciled with God!). Can you use Jesus as your example and empty yourself of any pride so that your relationship can be restored? Jesus was perfect. Yet, He took it upon himself to initiate reconciliation between us and God through His atoning sacrifice on the cross.

Ephesians 4:32 says, "Be kind and compassionate to one another, forgiving each other, just as in Christ God forgave you."

Pray for the Holy Spirit to guide you and reach out to that person. Don't allow yourself to be a doormat, but do be okay with loving them unconditionally, even if they don't return it. You can't control how they will respond but know that you made your Heavenly Father smile with your effort.

TUESDAY – DAY SIX

NANCY GOLDEN

I was visiting a friend whose husband was struck by a car when riding his bicycle. He was in a coma for several weeks, and we have been praying for his restoration. This visit was joyful, for he had come out of the coma and was making slow and steady progress. As we chatted, my friend made a comment that stood out to me. She said that it is through suffering that we are able to experience joy. Such a profound statement!

In other words, there is no measure for joy unless one understands what it means to be without joy. If you live a life untroubled by trials, you lead a bland existence. While this does not necessarily sound like a bad thing (who willingly wants to experience suffering?), it is those who have truly experienced the darkest of days that understand the gift of joy with an appreciation to the depths of their soul.

Paul writes in Romans 8:18, "I consider that our present sufferings are not worth comparing with the glory that will be revealed in us." How exciting it is to be a Christ-follower! Our future is assured.

Jesus tells us in John 16:33, "I have told you these things, so that in me you may have peace. In this world you will have trouble. But take heart! I have overcome the world." This verse tells us we will have trouble, and that suffering is inevitable. But He goes a step further to give us incredible peace. Jesus has already assured us a place of joy if we follow Him. And all the more, we will experience that joy to the full, having persevered through the suffering of our earthly existence.

Life is made up of contrasts. To truly understand one state, one must experience the opposite state. As we journey through Lent, let us reflect on our dire need for Christ as we acknowledge our sinful state and repent. But also rejoice, for God promises to redeem us through His Son and save us from ourselves – so that we may experience everlasting joy with the glory that is coming. Hallelujah!

$$\sim$$

TODAY'S ACTIVITY: Can you recall a time when you felt hopeless? How did you respond?

Memorize 1 Peter 5:7, "Cast all your anxiety on him because he cares for you." The next time you begin to feel without hope – remind yourself of that verse. God's care is a deep, active involvement in your welfare! Recall the assurance in John 16:33 that despite the fact we will have trouble in this world, Jesus has the final victory. Hang on tight to your Savior!

WEDNESDAY – DAY SEVEN

NANCY GOLDEN

This is the one time I am permitting myself to publish a devotional from the first book in my series, Taking Back Advent, and that is because I think it is so important. Biblical hope is our topic.

As we await our Lord Jesus with excitement and anticipation, we are filled with hope. What a joy it is to be a Christ-follower! As we travel through life as temporary inhabitants of this world, we know where our true citizenship lies. "Biblical hope" is much different from how we usually use the word "hope" in our day-to-day conversations. Have you ever said, "I hope to get a raise?" or "I hope we can go to the beach on vacation next year?" or "I hope they have that shirt in my size?" All of those statements imply uncertainty—there is no guarantee that what we are hoping for will come to fruition.

Biblical hope is not like that. It is not based on circumstances but rather on the promises and character of God. This hope is not a wishful, uncertain desire, but a confident certainty and a blessed assurance for those who follow Christ. Paul writes in Romans 5:3-4, "And not only this, but we also glory in our sufferings, knowing that suffering produces perseverance; perseverance, character; and character, hope;"

Paul uses the Greek word ἐλπίς [transliterated as elpis] in this verse. It is the hope we have in Jesus as our Risen Lord who has overcome death. While we travel through the difficulties of a broken world, we are joyful and have a confident expectation of eternal salvation.

We look back to the Resurrection and are filled with joy at the hope we have in Him. Easter is a time of family gatherings, and of visiting with friends and relatives. It is also the perfect time to share the hope you have with others so that they, too, can have the blessed assurance you have.

TODAY'S ACTIVITY: Can you think of someone within your sphere of influence with whom you can share the hope you have? Be sensitive to the leading of the Holy Spirit and be prepared for spiritual conversations. One of my favorite conversation starters is to say, "Christmas is my second favorite holiday of the year," which inevitably leads to the question, "Well, what's your first?" What a great opportunity to explain the hope we have in the Resurrection on Easter Sunday!

THURSDAY – DAY EIGHT

NANCY GOLDEN

As we reflect on our journey during this solemn season of repentance, it's easy to get caught up in our regrets. My sister-in-law likes to say that we are experiential learners, and I think that is so true. I look back on my life, and sometimes, when I examine it closely, I feel overwhelmed with what I could have done differently.

It is not always because I gave in to the temptation of sin. Sometimes, I feel heartbroken because I just didn't know any better. I think when we talk about repentance, these two are intertwined. We can feel deep regret, even shame, for responding to a situation when—at the time—we thought we had the right response. Empathy and wisdom are some things that grow with life experience and maturity.

I can identify my sins and ask my Father in Heaven for forgiveness, but what do I do with my feelings of regret and shame when I could have done better but didn't know how? I think that is part of the human condition. When we recognize those feelings, we should ask forgiveness for those past regrets, but we should also try to then release them. Lay our sorrows at the foot of the cross where our Savior died to take away our sin and shame. And then do better.

I really like the words of Maya Angelou, a famous writer, poet, and civil rights activist. If you haven't heard of her, you may want to find out more about her. I find many of her quotes very inspiring, and this one is especially appropriate for our topic today:

"Do the best you can until you know better. Then when you know better, do better."

And that is the solution to our problem of being experiential learners. While it won't fix the problem of not responding as well as we could have due to ignorance or immaturity (There will always be some things we don't know simply because we haven't had the opportunity to learn about them), it will instill in us an approach that honors God and people to the best of our ability. This won't be a stagnant exercise – as you increase in understanding, so will you enable yourself to respond with love and empathy in increasing measure to those around you.

TODAY'S ACTIVITY: Reflect on 2 Peter 1:5-8: "For this very reason, make every effort to add to your faith goodness; and to goodness, knowledge; and to knowledge, self-control; and to self-control, perseverance; and to perseverance, godliness; and to godliness, mutual affection; and to mutual affection, love. For if you possess these qualities in increasing measure, they will keep you from being ineffective and unproductive in your knowledge of our Lord Jesus Christ."

Notice in verse 8 that Peter writes, "For if you possess these qualities in increasing measure." We are all on a journey that started when we received Jesus as our Lord and Savior, and we cultivate these qualities as we learn and grow in our faith. Let us strive each day to become more like Him.

FRIDAY – DAY NINE

NANCY GOLDEN

Last night, I lay in bed thinking about God and my relationship with Him. During the Lenten season, our thoughts turn to our need for forgiveness and the fact that Jesus died on the cross to take away our sins so that we can spend eternity with Him. The words of the Roman Catholic liturgy, Agnus Dei, come to mind:

> Lamb of God, who takes away the sins of the world, have mercy on us.
> Lamb of God, who takes away the sins of the world, have mercy on us.
> Lamb of God, who takes away the sins of the world, grant us peace.

This prayer is based on John 1:29, when John the Baptist, upon seeing Jesus, exclaims, "Behold, the Lamb of God, who takes away the sin of the world!" To explain a bit further, Jesus is the sacrificial Lamb, rooted in the Jewish tradition of sacrifice for atonement. He is the ultimate fulfillment of the sacrificial system, and as the Agnus Dei reflects, He offers us mercy and peace through His sacrifice.

I found myself thinking of my sin and my desperate state, in need of God's forgiveness. Usually, when I pray after going to bed, I typically do so while under the covers. But last night, I found myself in the dark, kneeling at my bedside. I cried out silently for God to forgive me of my sins. I didn't stay there long, but that simple act made me feel better.

It is good to remember that God is the Creator, and we are the created. We owe everything to Him, and while He is worthy of our adoration and praise, He is also worthy of our obedience and submission.

TODAY'S ACTIVITY: God gave us an incredible gift—He allows us to converse with Him! Repentance is both ceasing to engage in sinful acts, and also asking our Heavenly Father to forgive us when we do, with a contrite heart. He promises that once He forgives us, He remembers our sins no more. Psalm 103:12 says, "as far as the east is from the west, so far has he removed our transgressions from us."

We can be assured that once we are forgiven, we are held blameless for that sin. But we must do our part, acknowledge our sins before Him, and ask Him to forgive us. I think that when we do that, God will answer the prayer of the Agnus Dei, take away our sins, and grant us peace.

Take a few minutes to be still and search your heart. Is there something you need to talk to your Heavenly Father about today? Even better, set aside time each day to reflect on anything you may need to ask forgiveness for and bring them to your Heavenly Father—a great way to engender peace to your days!

SATURDAY – DAY TEN

NANCY GOLDEN

We like to think we are pretty good people, but when we are truthful with ourselves, we see our sin exposed under the light of the Gospel. While this is undoubtedly an unfortunate state—praise God that we are not left without hope. The good news is that Jesus gives us His righteousness when we accept His gift of eternal life by believing in Him.

So, what is sin? I have heard many different definitions. Sin is missing the mark, which is God's standard for us. Sin is a willful transgression of a known law of God. I was thinking about that this morning, and I concluded that the entire basis of sin is when we think about ourselves rather than thinking about God and others.

The two greatest commandments that Jesus gives us are found in Matthew 22:37-39, "'Love the Lord your God with all your heart and with all your soul and with all your mind.' This is the first and greatest commandment. And the second is like it: 'Love your neighbor as yourself.'" Notice that it points us away from ourselves and towards God and others.

I must admit I was discouraged when I created a digital card for a person who had suffered a traumatic injury. The card was such that you could click on the link and easily write a note to the person to encourage them and sign your name. When the person receives the link, they click on it and view a card with a bunch of "thinking of you" notes attached. Working remotely, this is a great way to give someone a card that everyone can sign. My discouragement came not from the many people who wrote wonderful notes of affirmation for this person but rather from those few who refused.

To continue this thought, people may say they do not feel led or called to do something. Now, I can understand if they don't feel called to be a missionary overseas, which is a huge undertaking that should be pursued carefully with prayer and discernment. But they don't feel called to spend less than five minutes writing a note that would encourage somebody who faced a life-threatening illness? Is it about them? Maybe they don't like the person – should that stop them from doing something for someone in need? Matthew 5:47 tells us, "If you are kind only to your friends, how are you different from anyone else? Even pagans do that."

In Romans 3:23, we learn we all have sinned and fallen short, and we surely do. We are human and frail, and we don't always respond perfectly. But let's challenge ourselves to do better. The simple act of writing a note that would perhaps encourage a person should be the focus, and not about how well we get along with them. Lent is a time focused on repentance. Let us do as Paul writes in Philippians 2:3, "Do nothing from selfish ambition or conceit, but in humility count others more significant than yourselves."

～

TODAY'S ACTIVITY: Can you think of an area that you could have done better? I did today. I know someone in a nursing home who left me a phone message a few days ago, "just to say hi." But to be completely honest, I know it is more than that. They are probably feeling lonely and would like more visitors. I have resolved to go see him next week.

Who may you be neglecting, just because it hasn't been convenient, or perhaps, you simply don't feel that connected with them? I had to stop making it all about me and ask myself, "What would Jesus want me to do?" Do you have a similar situation in your life? Perhaps it's time to ask yourself the same question.

SUNDAY – GUEST DEVOTIONAL

PHIL GOLDEN

In 1 Corinthians 13:13, the Apostle Paul writes, "So now faith, hope, and love abide, but the greatest of these is love." This Lenten Season, I invite you to reflect and contemplate the depth of God's love for you.

How can we be assured of God's love for us? First and foremost, His Word, the Bible, says so:

John 3:16 states, "For God so loved the world that he gave his one and only Son, that whoever believes in him shall not perish but have eternal life."

Additionally, consider these as tangible evidence of God's love:

- The many blessings God has bestowed on you. Take some time and count them!
- The beauty of God's creation. Open your eyes and admire the evidence all around you.
- The people God places in your life. God brings people into your life to love and encourage you and to provide you with opportunities to share the Gospel.

- The blessings of friends to converse with and confide in.
- The ability you have to help others. Whether you're healthy or facing medical challenges, you have the ability to be an example of God's love to others. If you cannot help someone physically, you can always pray for them.
- By giving you a Bible to read. Read, heed, and share His Word. God loves you and everyone you come into contact with.

Matthew 6:26 reminds us, "Look at the birds of the air; they do not sow or reap or store away in barns, and yet your heavenly Father feeds them. Are you not much more valuable than they?"

1 John 4:9-11 explains, "This is how God showed his love among us: He sent his one and only Son into the world that we might live through him. This is love: not that we loved God, but that he loved us and sent his Son as an atoning sacrifice for our sins. Dear friends, since God so loved us, we also ought to love one another."

God loves us so much, He sent His only Son to die in our place so we can have eternal life! 1 John also emphasizes the importance of loving others. Be intentional in showing love to everyone you meet, whether it's a kind word to your server, a smile to a passerby, or a simple "God bless you" to others.

Acknowledge others for all they do for you. You never know the positive impact a simple "Thank you" may have on someone who is feeling discouraged.

∾

TODAY'S ACTIVITY: Pray for divine guidance in these acts of love:

- Take a moment to call or text someone you may have had a troubled relationship with and let them know how much you care about them. Especially think about those people in your life that you may have some conflict or disagreement with. Even though you don't see eye to eye – make sure they know you love them despite your differences.
- Be intentional about letting a friend know how much they mean to you by expressing your love and appreciation for their friendship.
- Purchase a card or gift for someone whom God puts on your heart.
- Share and show the love of God, pass it on.

MONDAY – DAY ELEVEN

NANCY GOLDEN

Our lives are incredibly busy. How did we get here? More importantly, how can we be intentional about slowing down? God created the Sabbath because He knew we needed rest. He also desires us to spend time with Him. Lent is a great time to reflect on our busyness and remind ourselves to slow down.

My husband Phil and I took my mother to visit a doctor for a second opinion a few years ago. We didn't see Mom as often as we would have liked since she lived in another city and our schedules were quite full. Mom didn't drive anymore and didn't get out much. Because the distances involved in traveling to her house and taking her to the doctor (which was in a city in the opposite direction) would entail us driving over a hundred miles by the time we were done, Phil decided to take the morning off. His plan was to return to work after the doctor's appointment, which would be around mid-afternoon.

But something happened along the way. God has a way of reminding us what is really important. Rather than going to the appointment and bringing Mom straight home afterward, after leaving the doctor's office, we decided to take her to a nice restaurant and spend the afternoon over a late leisurely lunch. We all had a wonderful time with delicious food and great conversation, and it was so lovely to see Mom enjoying herself.

After we took Mom home and got her settled back into her cozy house, we got in the car to begin our trek back home. Phil and I spent the drive time going over the day's events. Something that Phil said really stood out to me. He shared with me what had changed his mind about rushing back to work after Mom's appointment.

Phil recalled someone he knew who—at church during worship time—would constantly flip the pages forward to the next hymn before the one being sung was finished. Phil said, "It always bothered me that she did that." His point was that we need to experience the hymn we are singing rather than being so task-oriented that we rush forward and look for the next one before we are even finished with the one we are in. Phil explained that when we were with Mom, he realized that he needed to pause and enjoy the hymn he was in rather than rush forward to the next one.

The afternoon with Mom was the opportunity for a beautiful hymn that God provided to be enjoyed. Phil could either ignore the opportunity—missing out on the beauty of enjoying the present moment and spending time with Mom—or he could fully enjoy all of the choruses of the hymn. Ultimately, God was much more pleased with Phil's choice: investing time in my mother, showing her His love by staying and enjoying the entire hymn with her.

We can draw a lesson from the time Jesus spent in the wilderness: slow down. Just as Jesus spent time with His Father, we can do likewise and enjoy the hymn we are in.

∾

TODAY'S ACTIVITY: If you are like me, your days are filled with tasks to be completed. As soon as I get caught up in one area, more things to be done appear on the horizon. It is so easy to get caught up rushing to the next hymn in the hymnal that we don't pause to enjoy the hymn that we are in.

Let's stop and ask ourselves, "Is there a neighbor I need to check on? Is there a friend I have not talked to in a while? Is there someone I have meant to get in touch with that I haven't made time for? When was the last time I went with our teenage son or daughter for a walk in the park, to the library, or a breakfast outing?"

All of these are hymns that we can immerse ourselves in if we choose. While there is a degree of necessity in doing many tasks, it is how we prioritize our day that allows us to make room for the hymns of life that are truly meaningful.

TUESDAY – DAY TWELVE

NANCY GOLDEN

Not only during this season of repentance, but in general, I often struggle with feelings of regret. I keep thinking I could have done things better. This hits me hardest when I think about those I love who have gone on to be with the Lord. I don't have another chance with them to do better—I just have to wait until I see them in Heaven. Did I do enough for my mom while she was here on Earth? Did I make her feel loved and valued?

I know I could have made a greater effort to spend more time with her. I can't blame it all on being a mom to my own kids and all of the work I was doing, even though my mom made it clear she understood. Looking back, I could have done more, and I still wrestle with that. I can apply those thoughts to other people I care about that have gone to be with the Lord as well.

I must say, it is a terrible burden to carry. But then I remember something that is really the most important thing. We can't be perfect in our human endeavors. It simply isn't possible. If we were perfect, God would not have needed to help us find a way out from our sins. Our righteousness before God is perfect because it is imparted to us from the atoning work Jesus did on our behalf on the cross.

There is an old saying—Hindsight is 20/20. In other words, when we look back on our lives, we can see clearly what we have done and where we could have done better. But living in the moment, we don't see nearly as clearly. The question is, are we doing the best we can with what we know at the moment we are in? I think sometimes we need to give ourselves grace. A more mature version of ourselves may be tempted to answer no— because we look back through a lens tempered by the wisdom that life brings as we age. But perhaps the answer is yes—I did— for the moment I was in. We can't see the future, and we are not perfect, so we live in a tension of what to do in each moment.

Remember Maya Angelou's words we considered in Day Eight? "Do the best you can until you know better. Then, when you know better, do better." If we can do that, it can help us come to a place of peace.

I am quite sure that my mom is not at all worried about where I fell short—for she is in her new body, experiencing the joy of Heaven and being in the presence of her Savior. So when the devil tries to steal my own joy by attacking me with thoughts of regret, I just need to remind myself that:

A. I have asked my Heavenly Father for forgiveness; He remembers my sin no more (Isaiah 43:25)—so why should I?

B. While I have on occasion given in to selfishness and have not always done my best, I need to offer myself grace and recognize my own frail humanity.

C. Now, I can do better.

The enemy comes to rob, steal, and destroy. As a Christ follower—we have power over the devil. Don't let him win—give yourself grace for not being perfect and be grateful for the grace that God extends to us through His Son, Jesus Christ, so that we are not condemned (Romans 8:1: "There is therefore now no condemnation for those who are in Christ Jesus"). Learn from past mistakes and do better.

TODAY'S ACTIVITY: Think about how you can respond if you find yourself in a spiral of past regret. Be intentional. If you, like me, have some regrets regarding a past relationship, write down in a notebook the positive things that occurred during your time together and focus on those. When you start having negative thoughts, you can open the notebook and remind yourself of the blessings rather than dwelling on the sorrows.

WEDNESDAY – DAY THIRTEEN

NANCY GOLDEN

We sometimes wrestle with our sinful state. Even as new creations in Christ, we find ourselves giving in to our flesh. While we can't help uncharitable or inappropriate thoughts, which are Satan's arrows being sent our way, how we respond to them determines if we will give in to the temptation to sin.

Sometimes, I fail in my response, dwell on those thoughts, and amplify them. On my worst days, I may also participate in actively gossiping. Scripture warns us against making demeaning remarks about others:

Proverbs 16:28, "A perverse person stirs up conflict, and a gossip separates close friends."

Ephesians 4:29, "Do not let any unwholesome talk come out of your mouths, but only what is helpful for building others up according to their needs, that it may benefit those who listen."

I am using gossip as one of many examples of where we can fall into sin. When we accepted Jesus as our Lord and Savior, we became justified before God. It is because of the righteousness of Jesus that we receive our salvation, and not through our own efforts—which would be impossible. We do not have the capacity to be "good enough" on our own. Through the capacity of God's goodness through His Son's perfect sacrifice on the cross to atone for our sins (past, present, and future), we can stand before our holy God and enter paradise on the day He calls us to our eternal home.

In response, with grateful hearts, we begin a journey that is referred to as sanctification—a journey where we become more Christ-like as we mature in our faith. However, that does not mean we are suddenly transformed into perfect beings who never sin. Jesus was fully human and fully God when He left the heavenly realms to live among us—He is the only human who did not sin.

Know that our Heavenly Father has great compassion for us. If we wrestle with sin at times (and we will), we do not lose our salvation as a consequence. If we were perfect, we wouldn't need a Savior. God knows that, which is why He provided His Son, in the greatest sacrifice of all, to cover our sins. The antidote to our struggle with sin is the grace of God.

So, how should we respond when we find that we have failed in our effort not to sin? The title of Kyle Matthews' song gives us a telling observation of the Christian life, "We Fall Down." But the song goes on to describe that we get up again—by the power of God, who forgives us. Proverbs 24:16 says, "for though the righteous fall seven times, they rise again," to encourage us.

Keep in mind that the number seven is not meant in the literal sense—but in the Bible, it reflects perfection or completion. We fall down, but we get up—no matter how many times we sin. God will extend His grace and compassion and forgive us no matter how often we mess up. He loves us that much!

TODAY'S ACTIVITY: Memorize Philippians 4:8, "Finally, brothers and sisters, whatever is true, whatever is noble, whatever is right, whatever is pure, whatever is lovely, whatever is admirable—if anything is excellent or praiseworthy—think about such things."

Whenever you find yourself being tempted by unwholesome thoughts, remind yourself of this verse. Having it at the ready will help you follow Paul's guidance when temptations arise. And if you fall – get back up. God's forgiveness is always available to those with repentant hearts. It's good to remind ourselves that if we were perfect – we wouldn't need Jesus.

THURSDAY – DAY FOURTEEN

NANCY GOLDEN

Do you ever get caught up thinking about something from your past that you regret and find yourself reliving the guilt and shame—so much so that it plagues you and robs you of your joy? We know that God forgives our sins when we ask, and we can even forgive others, but sometimes, we struggle to forgive ourselves and release our guilty feelings.

Amazing grace is exactly that—AMAZING! But you need to accept it and live in its reality. My prayer for you is to stop shouldering that guilt. None of us are perfect; indeed, we are each born into sin. God's grace rescues us from that sorry state, but we must let it!

If you are experiencing feelings of guilt from sin that you have already confessed, trust the promises of God that He has forgiven your sin and removed your guilt – the atoning blood of Christ has already cleansed you. 1 John 1:9 tells us, "If we confess our sins, He is faithful and just and will forgive us our sins and purify us from all unrighteousness," and Romans 8:1 assures us that "Therefore, there is now no condemnation for those who are in Christ Jesus." Ask the Lord to rebuke Satan and restore the joy that comes with freedom from guilt.

When you begin to feel guilty over past sins you have already confessed, repented of, and have been forgiven, realize that this is Satan, the accuser, and reject those feelings as false guilt. The Lord is true to His promise to forgive. Psalm 103:8-12 tells us,

> The LORD is compassionate and gracious,
>> slow to anger, abounding in love.
>> He will not always accuse,
>> nor will He harbor his anger forever;
>> he does not treat us as our sins deserve
>> or repay us according to our iniquities.
>> For as high as the heavens are above the earth,
>> so great is his love for those who fear him;
>> as far as the east is from the west,
>> so far has He removed our transgressions from us.

If possible, follow Zacchaeus's example of reparation in Luke 19:8. Sometimes, guilt remains because personal reconciliation is no longer possible. Perhaps it involves a broken relationship or a person who has gone on to be with the Lord, so that there is nothing you can do to make up for your transgression. That is when you need to bring your feelings to the Lord and ask Him to provide peace and healing so that you can move on.

Remember that you are a new creation—the old is gone—including feelings of guilt and regret. Your sins have been forgiven! God is more concerned with your present than your past and wants you to live in victory as a child of God.

∾

TODAY'S ACTIVITY: 2 Corinthians 9:8 tells us, "And God is able to make all grace abound to you, so that having all sufficiency in all things at all times, you may abound in every good work." Put your focus on serving God's kingdom rather than allowing guilt to render you ineffective.

John 8:36 tells us, "So if the Son sets you free, you will be free indeed." Jesus went to the cross for all of us to pay the price for our sin—make a focused effort to turn loose of your guilt and let God's grace wash over you today! Pray this simple prayer every time those guilty feelings begin to return:

HEAVENLY FATHER, thank you for cleansing me from all guilt and shame through the grace of your Son, Jesus Christ, who took on the burden of my sin so that I can be free. Help me to only listen to Your voice and live in the truth of Your promises. Amen.

FRIDAY – DAY FIFTEEN

NANCY GOLDEN

D o you ever feel like a prodigal? Not necessarily in a literal sense, but perhaps a figurative one. I know I do. I am not spending my father's inheritance foolishly like the younger son in Luke's Gospel, but sometimes I find myself not behaving as a child of God should. I say the wrong thing. I give in to temptation. I don't spend time in my Bible. I am prideful. I get really mad. I don't offer to help. Any transgression, big or small, is an affront to God's holiness. These transgressions can cause us to feel far from our Heavenly Father. Paul speaks to this aspect of the human condition in Romans 7:14-25:

> We know that the law is spiritual; but I am unspiritual, sold as a slave to sin. I do not understand what I do. For what I want to do I do not do, but what I hate I do. And if I do what I do not want to do, I agree that the law is good. As it is, it is no longer I myself who do it, but it is sin living in me. For I know that good itself does not dwell in me, that is, in my sinful nature. For I have the desire to do what is good, but I cannot carry it out. For I do not do the good I want to do, but the evil I do not want to

do—this I keep on doing. Now if I do what I do not want to do,
it is no longer I who do it, but it is sin living in me that does it.

I love the story of the prodigal son found in the Gospel of
Luke, Chapter 15:11-32, because it is a rich tale that speaks to
God's relationship with us, represented by the father in the story.
It is one of the most beautiful passages in Scripture, and it starts
with a son who asks his father prematurely for his inheritance,
and when the father gives it to him, the son squanders it on a
sinful lifestyle. When he runs out of money and has nowhere
else to go, he decides to return home and plans to ask his father
to allow him to be one of his father's servants, so that he may
have a place to sleep and food to eat. The father's response is
one of astonishing and extravagant grace. Upon seeing his son
approaching, Scripture tells us in Luke 15:20:

"And he arose and came to his father. But while he was still a
long way off, his father saw him and felt compassion, and ran
and embraced him and kissed him."

Imagine that in your mind's eye! The Lord over all creation
RAN to embrace His lost son. The fact that God loves us that
much—that when we turn (or return) to Him—He is there
waiting with open arms and will run to meet us and take us into
His embrace, should take our breath away with amazement and
gratitude.

Have you not been behaving as a child of God? Have you
wandered astray and are ready to come home? There is no need
to worry about your reception. Your Heavenly Father is waiting
with hopeful anticipation and wide, open arms. As soon as He
sees you coming—He will run to meet you. He will forgive your
sins and envelop you in His extravagant love. Why wait another
moment? Come home today!

～

TODAY'S ACTIVITY: "When God Ran" is a powerful song by Benny Hester that speaks to the prodigal and gives reassurance of God's grace. It has been performed by both Benny Hester and Phillips, Craig, and Dean. Find it on YouTube (either version) and make some time in your day to listen to it.

Soak in the words, and in your mind's eye, imagine your Heavenly Father running toward you with open arms. Run into His embrace and allow His love to wash over you. Know you are forgiven. Know that you are a child of God. Know that you are loved beyond measure.

SATURDAY – DAY SIXTEEN

NANCY GOLDEN

S cripture tells us we were born into sin. So how do we avoid it? We live in a broken world, and temptations are all around us. We must fight our sinful nature, and we are constantly under assault. What can we do to resist the attacks of the evil one?

Paul gives us the answer in Ephesians 6:10-18:

Finally, be strong in the Lord and in his mighty power. Put on the full armor of God, so that you can take your stand against the devil's schemes. For our struggle is not against flesh and blood, but against the rulers, against the authorities, against the powers of this dark world and against the spiritual forces of evil in the heavenly realms. Therefore, put on the full armor of God, so that when the day of evil comes, you may be able to stand your ground, and after you have done everything, to stand. Stand firm then, with the belt of truth buckled around your waist, with the breastplate of righteousness in place, and with your feet fitted with the readiness that comes from the gospel of peace. In addition to all this, take up the shield of faith, with which you can extinguish all the flaming arrows of the evil one. Take the helmet of salvation and the sword of the Spirit, which is the word of God.

And pray in the Spirit on all occasions with all kinds of prayers and requests. With this in mind, be alert and always keep on praying for all the Lord's people.

God provides His spiritual armor for each one of us. We fight from victory through the Resurrection of our Lord Jesus, who conquered death:

1 Corinthians 15:55-57,

Where, O death, is your victory?

Where, O death, is your sting?

The sting of death is sin, and the power of sin is the law. But thanks be to God! He gives us the victory through our Lord Jesus Christ.

Jesus has already provided our victory, but we need to wear our spiritual armor daily so that we can be effective and stand firm against the attacks of the enemy. We can't always stop spiritual assaults, but we can make sure our spiritual armor is in place to protect us.

During this Lenten season, we realize our mortality, but we are not vulnerable. Remember that our God goes before us and provides us with spiritual protection.

TODAY'S ACTIVITY: Create a daily morning routine that allows you to read Ephesians 6:10-18. As you read each verse out loud, imagine yourself putting on each piece of armor. Move through your day with confidence, and when one of Satan's darts comes your direction, deflect it by acknowledging the spiritual protection you have in place.

Live in the promise of Romans 8:11, "And if the Spirit of him who raised Jesus from the dead is living in you, he who raised Christ from the dead will also give life to your mortal bodies because of his Spirit who lives in you." The victory has already been won through our Lord Jesus Christ!

SUNDAY – GUEST DEVOTIONAL

KATHLEEN BALDWIN

"Good is my rock, in whom I take refuge, my shield, and the horn of my salvation, my stronghold and my refuge, my savior; you save me from violence." 2 Samuel 22:3

"He is my loving ally and my fortress, my tower of safety, my rescuer. He is my shield, and I take refuge in him. He makes the nations submit to me." Psalm 144:2

243 verses in the Old and New Testament speak of the Lord rescuing/delivering/protecting His people. Rescuer and Savior, our Lord Jesus is both, but there is a critical distinction.

Long before I fully understood salvation, I knew the Lord as my refuge and rescuer.

During my teenage years, I became an avid rock climber and loved being out in the wilderness. I felt closest to God in the quiet of remote deserts and mountain forests. So, I would often go out in the wilderness by myself survival camping without food, a sleeping bag, or a tent. You can probably imagine how often the Lord protected me from falls, scorpions, snakes, and mountain lions. For instance, one morning, I woke up high up in the Rocky Mountains after sleeping beneath a shallow rock outcropping and discovered a mountain lion had made a fresh kill that night and eaten it only three yards from where I slept.

I felt saved—but the truth is I'd been rescued over and over and over. I loved Him for those countless rescues, and yet I still hadn't fully understood that the greatest danger I faced was eternal death. A mountain lion was nothing compared to eternal death. A 60-foot fall off a cliff was minuscule pain in comparison to suffering for my sins throughout eternity.

It wasn't until I felt the heavy consequences of my sins that I began to understand my need for eternal salvation. I sinned big. And although I repented and kept trying to make up for my sin, I never felt truly forgiven. This was because I didn't understand grace.

Romans 4: 4-5: "Now to the one who works, his wages are not counted as a gift but as his due. And to the one who does not work but believes in him who justifies the ungodly, his faith is counted as righteousness."

I'd been unwittingly trying to be virtuous enough, to do good enough, to be sorry enough to deserve God's forgiveness. Trying, trying, trying—but that was me working, and the wages I would've been paid were death.

The wages of sin are death. How was I going to work hard enough or be good enough to pay that price? Death. Thankfully, God sent teachers into my life to help me understand grace intellectually. Unfortunately, emotionally, I still couldn't fully grasp it.

God, in His mercy, sent a dream to help me understand the depth of His grace.

This dream felt so real that it hardly seemed like a dream at all. In it, Jesus and I were walking down a hallway, heading for some ominous wooden doors. The closer we got, the more I pleaded with Him not to go to that place. Finally, in a panic, I grasped His sleeve and made Him stop walking. "You can't go in there! The Sanhedrin is in there. They're going to kill You."

Jesus turned and leaned close to me—I'll never forget the love on His face and the kindness in His voice. "I have to go in there," He said, "for you." I sank back, completely undone. Stunned, mortified, overcome, I couldn't move. He walked away and glanced back with a gentle smile before opening those awful doors and walking through.

I understood in that terrible moment that He suffered and died for me. Not just all of humanity, Jesus died for me. And for you. Even if you and I were the only two people on earth, Jesus loves us so much that He would've done it just for the two of us.

TODAY'S ACTIVITY: A psalm is simply a song of praise or a written prayer of gratitude. It is the truth of how you feel right now about what the Lord has done for you. Some of David's psalms began with desperate pleas for help and complaints about the troubles surrounding him. But as he kept writing, the psalm turned to praise and ended with David feeling encouraged and sure of the Lord's Salvation and Rescue.

In light of Jesus's sacrifice for you, can you write a personal Psalm? This needn't be anything you show anyone else. It is between you and God. It would be a beautiful tribute. It doesn't have to be long or poetic. It is simply you pouring out your heart.

MONDAY – DAY SEVENTEEN

NANCY GOLDEN

J esus went into the wilderness to fast and pray, often regarded as a season of preparation for His earthly ministry. When we examine the example Jesus set for us, we can learn much about how to live and prepare for our own ministry in this world. I am not speaking specifically about formal ministry but recalling that we are all ambassadors of Christ (2 Corinthians 5:20), and as a priesthood of believers (1 Peter 2:9), we are all called to be ministers to a hurting world.

So, what are some lessons we can learn and apply in our own lives?

We read in the opening verses of Matthew Chapter 4:

Then Jesus was led by the Spirit into the wilderness to be tempted by the devil. And when He had fasted forty days and forty nights, He afterward hungered. And when the tempter came to Him, he said, "If Thou be the Son of God, command that these stones be made bread."

In verse 4, Jesus responds by quoting Deuteronomy 8:3:

Jesus answered, "It is written: 'Man shall not live on bread alone, but on every word that comes from the mouth of God.'"

We often forget this important truth – indeed, it is something that most of us struggle with – the desire for material objects. We believe if we have enough "stuff" (money, a bigger house, a nicer car), we will reach a place of contentment. None of these things will satisfy the yearnings of our hearts. We have a hole in our hearts that can only be filled by our Creator.

Rather than seeking financial wealth and earthly gain, let us focus on attaining spiritual wealth by growing in the knowledge of our Lord Jesus Christ and reflecting His love to those around us.

God will provide our daily bread, but our lives are about so much more. We glorify God by loving Him and those around us – our pursuit of accumulating wealth distracts us from what He created us to be, and we will never be satisfied as long as we pursue the things of this world.

TODAY'S ACTIVITY: Read Matthew 6:19-21 and reflect on where your own treasure lies. Define or re-examine your personal priorities. Make a list of what you would like to achieve and see how well it aligns with Matthew 22:34-40. Examine what is motivating you. Pray for discernment and guidance regarding any changes God may be calling you to make.

TUESDAY – DAY EIGHTEEN

NANCY GOLDEN

Yesterday, we looked at the first temptation of Jesus, as listed in Matthew 4:1-4. Today, we are going to look at the second temptation found in Matthew 4:5-6:

Then the devil took him to the holy city and had him stand on the highest point of the temple. "If you are the Son of God," he said, "throw yourself down. For it is written:

'He will command his angels concerning you, and they will lift you up in their hands, so that you will not strike your foot against a stone.'"

Satan is referencing Psalm 91:11-12. We can see that Satan is even willing to use Scripture to twist it for his own agenda. But Jesus knows better.

In the next verse, Matthew 4:7,

Jesus answered him, "It is also written: 'Do not put the Lord your God to the test.'"

Notice that Jesus again goes to Scripture (Deuteronomy 6:16) for His response. He knows Satan is trying to trick Him. Because Jesus knows the Scriptures, His response makes it obvious Satan is trying to manipulate Him by using them out of context, and He does not fall for Satan's lies. A good lesson for all of us!

We learned in an earlier devotional about the armor of God and the Bible in Ephesians 6:17, "Take the helmet of salvation and the sword of the Spirit, which is the word of God."

The Bible is the only offensive piece of armor mentioned; all the others are defensive – we have God's Word available to use as a weapon against the evil one, just as Jesus did when Satan tempted Him. Hebrews 4:12 says, "For the word of God is alive and active. Sharper than any double-edged sword, it penetrates even to dividing soul and spirit, joints and marrow; it judges the thoughts and attitudes of the heart."

TODAY'S ACTIVITY: As we have been learning from Jesus being tempted in the wilderness, the Word of God is an effective weapon (the sword of the Spirit in the armor of God) available to each of us to use for standing firm against Satan's attacks.

For example, one of my favorite verses for when I am feeling uncertain and worried about something is Proverbs 3:5. Since I have an engineering background, I often find myself trying to analyze a situation and the outcome. It could be as silly as passing someone who coughs. I start calculating how close I was and if they have COVID, did I get exposed?

I have learned to stop myself and to embrace Proverbs 3:5 instead, "Trust in the Lord with all your heart and lean not on your own understanding;" and by doing that, I remember that God is in control, regardless of what my mind may be saying. It is so much better to rest in God's provision and to trust Him in every situation.

Think about those areas in your life that seem especially troublesome. What temptations are specific to your own walk? Take some time to dive into the Bible and find some verses you can readily have available for when temptation comes. Follow Jesus' example - Learn Scripture (the sword in the armor of God) and have it at the ready.

WEDNESDAY – DAY NINETEEN

NANCY GOLDEN

Today, we will be looking at the third and final temptation that Jesus experienced in the wilderness as recorded in Scripture in Matthew 4:8-9:

> Again, the devil took him to a very high mountain and showed him all the kingdoms of the world and their splendor. "All this I will give you," he said, "if you will bow down and worship me."

Jesus turned to Scripture a third time, referencing Exodus 20:3, to respond in verse 10:

> Jesus said to him, "Away from me, Satan! For it is written: 'Worship the Lord your God, and serve him only.'"

God's own Son worshipped Him – how can we do any less? Isaiah 43:21 echoes God's purpose,

> the people I formed for myself
>   that they may proclaim my praise.

Satan tried to tempt Jesus with material gain. He does the same to all of us. He knows where we are weak. Remember that the Creator of the universe has you in mind—He wants to be in a relationship with YOU! When you worship the One deserving of all honor and praise, you are living your purpose in life. Revelation 4:11,

> You are worthy, O Lord,
>> To receive glory and honor and power;
>> For You created all things,
>> And by Your will they exist and were created.

Amassing power and wealth, while tempting, will not fulfill your purpose. Worshipping God and serving Him will fulfill your true purpose – and you will find that in doing so, God will provide for you the desires of your heart and you will live life more abundantly than you could ever imagine for yourself (Ephesians 3:20).

TODAY'S ACTIVITY: What are some things in your life you are pursuing? Perhaps a material object, a position, or an award? Maybe a relationship or a job? Examine the worthiness of these things in your life and determine if they are becoming an idol, preventing you from putting God first. Recognize if this is happening (we will be doing a study on the word insidious in a future devotional) and take steps to come back into obedience to God, worshipping Him alone.

Look up Psalm 37:4, John 10:10, and Ephesians 3:20. Marvel at the gifts God gives His children who delight in Him.

THURSDAY – DAY TWENTY

NANCY GOLDEN

W hile Lent is a season of reflection, we might find ourselves mired in difficult and complex questions. Why do bad things happen to good people? Why is there suffering in the world? While there are no easy answers to these questions, there are some verses that can bring us a measure of comfort when bad things do happen. For me, three specific verses come to mind:

2 Corinthians 1:3-4,

> Praise be to the God and Father of our Lord Jesus Christ, the Father of compassion and the God of all comfort, who comforts us in all our troubles, so that we can comfort those in any trouble with the comfort we ourselves receive from God.

While walking through difficulties is not something we look forward to, we can be grateful for the fact that once we are on the other side, we can be an encouragement to those who are suffering similar circumstances because we have already been through it. We truly understand what they are going through. God will use us to bless others, and while we may wish we did not have that particular experience, it is a joy to be able to minister to others in such a powerful way to help them through it.

Romans 8:28,

> And we know that in all things God works for the good of those who love him, who have been called according to his purpose.

This verse gives us confidence that even when we can't find any good anywhere, God will be able to use every situation for His glory. I have found this to be true over and over again, although you would not have been able to convince me of it when I was in the midst of the battle. Hindsight is indeed 20/20.

Genesis 50:20 is Joseph's response to his brothers who had sold him into slavery,

> You intended to harm me, but God intended it for good to accomplish what is now being done, the saving of many lives.

God had a tremendous plan for Joseph's life, a plan that included saving Egypt and the surrounding areas from a dreadful famine. But he went through terrible times, including being thrown in prison, before becoming the second most powerful man in Egypt, next to Pharaoh. Throughout good times and bad, Joseph remained faithful and obedient, and God was with him in every situation.

The answer to the problem of evil and suffering is not to glibly quote these verses. As a matter of fact, that might hurt more than it helps. But studying the meaning of these verses in context and then applying them can provide a powerful reminder that while we can't always know why bad things happen, we can find tremendous comfort in knowing God has a plan that He is working out, even when we don't understand it.

Our job is to have faith and be obedient, and when we don't think we can do that on our own, we can turn to the One who promises to help us in Philippians 4:13, "I can do all this through him who gives me strength."

TODAY'S ACTIVITY: Get a copy of "The Hiding Place" by Corrie Ten Boom and begin reading it. As you do so, reflect on how Corrie reacted to her situation and what you can learn from her response to the most heart-rending of circumstances.

FRIDAY – DAY TWENTY-ONE

NANCY GOLDEN

As we continue our journey through Lent, we can be grateful that despite the solemnity of the season, we can always take joy in our salvation. An incident from a few years ago reminds me of the different seasons of life and God's provision in each. My husband Phil and I saw my neighbor Susan's adult son Robert in his driveway. I asked him how his mom was doing - Susan had been in the hospital twice for extended periods, and the last time I talked to her on the phone (the previous week), she was in a rehab facility. Robert shared with me the unexpected news that Susan had gone to be with our Lord.

Susan always loved to ask me to pray for her, and I am really glad that I got to pray for her during that last phone call. I am also really glad that Phil and I could comfort Robert, and pray for him as we huddled together in the driveway. God has given us such a tremendous gift in prayer. When we don't know what else to do, we can always pray, which is bi-directional. We worship God through prayer, and we receive His comfort through prayer.

Susan was the first neighbor I met when I bought our home

in 1994. When Phil and I married, our wedding had been very small. Susan was so excited to cook for an open house in our home to celebrate our marriage with friends and family. Over the years, I would see her in her back driveway and walk across the alley to chat. We had many conversations, and what always struck me about Susan was her perseverance. The storms of life were constant, yet she just trusted in the Lord and kept going.

She is with her Lord now, free from the pain that has plagued her body for years. I will miss her strength, which I found very inspiring, and her compassion for others even when she was in the midst of her own battles.

But I'm not done yet...

After spending some time with Robert, we walked back into the house, and I picked up my phone. I noticed I had a text from Vero, a young woman who is very precious to me. The text was a picture of her newborn son Leo, born that very morning. There was something poetic about receiving the news of Susan's death, and, in the next moment, receiving news of a new life: a picture of God's incredible plan for each of us.

We have hope in a baby's new life and all the possibilities before him. Yet, as Christians, we also have hope in death, for we are merely leaving our earthly bodies behind as we move into our new life as purely spiritual beings. Leo is beginning a new adventure, but so is Susan.

Romans 14:8 says, "If we live, we live for the Lord; and if we die, we die for the Lord. So, whether we live or die, we belong to the Lord." Thank you, Jesus, for the assurance that when we accept You as our Lord and Savior, whether we live or die, we are Yours!

∼

TODAY'S ACTIVITY: As Christ-followers, we have an incredible hope. We are truly Easter people, living in the hope of the Resurrection. Reflect on the words of Paul in Philippians 1:21, "For to me, to live is Christ and to die is gain." Heaven will be a more wonderful place, for we will be with our Savior in a place devoid of sin, sickness, and death. But in the meantime – focus on the good you can do now.

Matthew 5:16 tells us, "In the same way, let your light shine before others, that they may see your good deeds and glorify your Father in heaven." What good can you do today?

SATURDAY – DAY TWENTY-TWO

NANCY GOLDEN

L uke writes in Acts 3:19, "Repent, then, and turn to God, so that your sins may be wiped out, that times of refreshing may come from the Lord." This verse speaks to the importance of repentance – It is through our repentance from sin that we enter into a relationship with God.

While repentance is an essential foundation stone of daily Christian life, Lent is a season when we examine our need to repent in the bigger picture of what lies ahead, the atoning work of Jesus on our behalf. Repentance is our response to God's grace, offered to us through the sacrificial atonement of His Son on the cross. When we repent, we feel genuine remorse for our sins and decide to turn away from them – to make a fundamental change in our lives and do our best not to sin anymore. True repentance will be reflected in our actions. When we repent, we surrender ourselves to God's will rather than our own.

I want to share some notes I took from a message by Pastor Chad Burton of Living Word Global Church in Irving, Texas.

John the Baptist is a great example of what it means to live a life devoted to God. He refers to himself in Matthew 3:3:

This is he who was spoken of through the prophet Isaiah:

> A voice of one calling in the wilderness,
> "Prepare the way for the Lord,
> make straight paths for him."

John's identity is in Jesus – He can only answer who he is in relation to Jesus! Let us find our identity in Christ and in all He brings with Him. Our lives are about belonging to Jesus! Let us magnify the Lord and allow Him to be the center of our lives.

Pastor Chad also elaborated about repentance that day – I have several nuggets of treasure to share from his words:

When we hear the word "repent," today we think it's all about guilt, but it is wrapped up in forgiveness and new life – the past no longer applies. The people seeking John the Baptist at the Jordan came because of all their failures – Repentance brings forgiveness and pardon! Repent from despair!

Don't live haunted by sin – but be cleansed from it. Pastor Chad mentioned a baptism confessional from the 1600s:

> Whenever I fall into sin,
> With God's help, I will repent and return to the Lord.

Pastor Chad shared that we shouldn't focus on our badness but on God's goodness – refuse despair! Rather than viewing repentance as a guilt-ridden exercise – we can free ourselves from guilt through our repentance. It allows us to recognize our own desperate need for the mercy and forgiveness of God.

Repent and return to the Lord. Not guilt and hopelessness, but forgiveness and mercy are found in God's power to cleanse us. Lean on Him. His grace will surpass anything this world can offer. Believe in God's goodness more than our badness. Believe in God, repent, and find your identity in Jesus!

TODAY'S ACTIVITY: Read Luke 19:1-10. Consider Zacchaeus' response when he was convicted of his sin. Read how David responded in Psalm 51 when he sinned against God. Use these examples in Scripture to help you respond when you are in need of repentance, knowing you can rely on God's graciousness and mercy for forgiveness when you approach Him with a contrite heart.

Remember, our identity is in Jesus. Repentance from those things that tempt us may be difficult in our flesh, but we know that when we ask, God will strengthen us and help us to live lives that are pleasing to Him.

SUNDAY – GUEST DEVOTIONAL

D. BAILEY WYNNE

A s a Black child born to charismatic Pentecostal evangelists in the South, Lent was not on my radar until I was an adult. The ritual of putting a dark smudge on one's forehead as a religious adherence was as foreign to me as the idea of flying to the Moon on a spaceship.

It all seemed very somber and lacking any effusive joy, which the services of my local church provided in abundance. I knew that every funeral ended with the proclamation of how we all become dust and ashes, and I did not want something from the dead on my face. In addition, I could see no connection between ashes and the expected Resurrection of King Jesus.

However, as an adult, I began to see why some people saw this practice as a path to reflect on the sacrificial death of Christ and to meditate on the authenticity of the religious life they claimed to live. To do so with piety and humility, sincerely living in gratitude for the gift of eternal life by fasting and repentance, is admirable and worthy of the Lamb who was slain.

As an adult, I came to realize that Lent is not about the smudge on our heads, but the stain on our spiritual hearts. It is a season of reaffirming to die to sin, sacrificially giving the entirety of who we are to His will, and living purposefully to honor His life and death for us all.

My participation in Lent now involves fasting, without the application of ashes. Instead, I have created a new ritual that accompanies my time of giving up something I love (food/social media). I choose not just to honor the death of the Savior but to celebrate how that death provided an avenue for a new beginning for mankind, filled with the hope of a new birth in Christ and the joy that "we shall share, when we tarry there, none other has ever known!"

With that sweet song (In the Garden) ringing in my ears, I plant daffodils to remind me, not just of the gravity of the grave but of the beauty of the Resurrection. Ashes may symbolize death, but with His death came hope, and every bright yellow flower that comes forth in spring, stands tall as a reminder.

TODAY'S ACTIVITY: Reflect on your childhood. What has changed in how you participate in Easter observances today as an adult? Are you setting aside time to truly know His will for your life? Are you able to see the beauty of Jesus' sacrifice?

As the Scripture tells us, with death, there may be weeping, but joy comes in the spring with the Resurrection of the Savior. (Psalm 30:5)

Romans 6:9-11:

For we know that since Christ was raised from the dead, he cannot die again; death no longer has mastery over him. The death he died, he died to sin once and for all; but the life he lives, he lives to God. In the same way, count yourselves dead to sin but alive to God in Christ Jesus.

Take time to quiet the chatter of this world, resisting the pull of its calls to take us away from listening to the voice of the Master. Sit expectantly and wait for Him. In His presence is hope and redemption. (Psalm 130:5)

Scriptures to read and study as you carve out time to not only focus on the Word of God but to see the joyous promise of spring:

Romans 6:9. 1 Corinthians 6:14.

1 Corinthians 15:22. John 11:25. Psalm 143:8.

"In the Garden" (1912); C. Austin Miles, in the public domain.

MONDAY – TWENTY-THREE

NANCY GOLDEN

My husband and I visited a friend in a nursing home today (the same person I mentioned in an earlier devotional). We had met Brother Ricky when attending a church about 45 minutes from our home. Since we decided to find a church in our own community, we had not seen him in a few years and not since he had moved there.

Brother Ricky lay on a bed in a room he shared with another male resident, just a curtain dividing them. As my gaze fell upon him, I wasn't sure if it was Ricky or not – his appearance had changed quite a bit as old age crept in. But as soon as he opened his mouth and started speaking – I knew it was him. His characteristic "Praise the Lord," started our conversation.

As we chatted with Ricky, he mentioned he prays for the person on the other side of the curtain, other residents, and the workers whose job is to care for them. He shared stories of healing and hope from his prayers, always giving God the glory.

Ricky is in the midst of the wilderness – his wife has gone home to be with the Lord, and he finds himself living in a nursing home out of necessity since he can no longer care for himself. It would be tempting to look at his circumstances and sink into despair; instead, Ricky finds his joy in the Lord daily and shares it with those around him. He continues to be a minister of the Gospel and prays for those he meets.

What a fantastic example for all of us! This gentle and loving man of God reached out his hands and prayed fervently for us, our friends, and family, as he lay in bed.

As I reflect on what God would have me learn during this Lenten season – two things come to mind:

1. We can be joyful—no matter our circumstances—when we understand that the true source of our joy is our relationship with Jesus Christ.

2. We can always do ministry no matter where we are – Ricky prays for people while lying in a bed in a nursing home.

I am grateful for Brother Ricky – for his love and friendship, for his prayers, and for inspiring me to serve God in whatever capacity I am able.

TODAY'S ACTIVITY: Nursing homes are often difficult places for both residents and those who care for them, and they often feel they are in the wilderness, isolated from society.

Plan to take some time to visit a nursing home. Be an encouragement to the workers as you walk the halls and greet the residents with a warm smile. Ask the staff if there is someone who has not had visitors – perhaps you can bring some joy to a lonely resident.

You may be getting out of your comfort zone – but just think of what Jesus did for us - He left the comfort of Heaven so He could save us from our sins!

TUESDAY – DAY TWENTY-FOUR

NANCY GOLDEN

Holy living is an ongoing theme during Lent as we recognize our need to repent from sin. But how can we develop holy living into a lifestyle and not let worldly influences corrupt us? INSIDIOUS is defined as, "awaiting a chance to entrap, harmful but enticing, and developing so gradually as to be well established before becoming apparent."

INSIDIOUS is one of the scariest words in the English language - because you don't even realize it is happening! This can be unhealthy habits you develop over time, changes in perspective that aren't good—that you find yourself easily justifying, allowing others to influence your behavior in ways you would not have in the past, or taking on the opinions of friends without validating them for yourself through the lens of Scripture. All of these are very subtle and very dangerous to your spiritual formation and your relationship with the Lord. So, how can you guard against the insidious influences in your life?

Remember our study on the Armor of God on Day 16? This concept is so crucial that it is worth revisiting again. Ephesians 6:10-11 tells us, "Finally, be strong in the Lord and in his mighty power. Put on the full armor of God, so that you can take your stand against the devil's schemes."

Part of being strong in the Lord means standing firm against the insidious influences of this world. Your identity is in Christ, and the devil is waging a war against you. It is essential to recognize the nature of his attack so that you can be strong in God's strength and resist those influences that would affect the great plans God has for your life!

TODAY'S ACTIVITY: Have you established a morning ritual of putting on your spiritual armor to combat any spiritual assaults you may encounter in your day? If you are like me, you may have done so but started slipping after a while.

Find a visual (there are lots of images if you google Armor of God) and select one you find inspiring. Print it out and put it within easy reach for when you wake up in the morning. Use the visual as a guide and become more consistent in putting on God's armor, so you will be well-prepared to fight the insidious influences swirling around you.

WEDNESDAY – DAY TWENTY-FIVE

NANCY GOLDEN

During Lent, many of us find ourselves reaching for our Bible more frequently as we seek to strengthen our spiritual practices. A few years ago, when attending seminary, I explained to my son Josh what I had been learning in my hermeneutics class (just a fancy way of saying "How to Study the Bible").

I told him about the importance of discovering what the author intended to communicate rather than just taking the words at face value when reading the Bible. He was really struggling with why we should try to dig deeper when studying Scripture – why can't we just read it and let the Holy Spirit open up the meaning for us?

I told him that was certainly an option, and we often do that in devotional reading. But if we want to truly understand and convey the text to others, we need to go further and ensure we are not taking God's intended meaning and misinterpreting it. We don't want to take it out of context, and—worse yet—we don't want to misrepresent it to others just because we have heard someone else teach it a certain way, without verifying it for ourselves. The Berean Jews in Acts 17:10-12 are a great example of studying the Scriptures for themselves to make sure Paul and Silas spoke truth.

I gave Josh the following hypothetical example:

Let's say that the apostle Paul tells us in Scripture that we should not eat French fries. This seems like good advice since French fries are fried and not good for your health. God wants us to be healthy, so this prohibition in the 21st century makes perfect sense. But what if that isn't the real reason why Paul tells us not to eat French fries? What if, after studying the historical context, we find that eating French fries in biblical times was an essential part of pagan ceremonies focused on witchcraft and talking to spirits of the dead?

If we had not diligently studied the historical context of Paul's prohibition, we would have misinterpreted its theological principle. According to the author's intended meaning, eating French fries had nothing to do with preserving one's physical health and everything to do with preserving one's spiritual health.

So we have two choices. We can quit eating French fries (which is not a bad idea but not the true meaning of Paul's words), or we can understand what Paul would have really meant: guard against engaging in any practices that flirt with the occult. How do we apply that in today's context? For instance, playing with an Ouija board— which many view purely as entertainment—is a very dangerous activity. Paul's admonition against French fries would apply to Ouija boards today.

Keep in mind that this example is made up – there is no prohibition against eating French fries in Scripture or any evidence that it is a pagan practice (although Ouija boards are spiritually dangerous and Scripture warns against their use in Deuteronomy 18:10-12).

It does illustrate my point: Digging deeper is not always easy, but it is sure to reveal much treasure in your studies that can tremendously impact how you interpret and apply what you read.

It's a few years later and it gladdens this mother's heart that Josh has embraced Inductive Bible Study in his own study of Scripture. You'll get to enjoy the fruits of his labor in the next guest devotional.

TODAY'S ACTIVITY: While today's example of French-fry-eating witches is hypothetical, the principle being conveyed is not. Inductive Bible Study principles are a great way to deepen your Bible Study.

Inductive Bible Study is being observant of the words in the passage and their place in the Scripture, capturing their historical and literary significance, and interpreting their meaning from the information flowing from your observations using sound Bible reference tools, and then applying what you have learned – allowing the Scripture to transform your life. Inductive Bible Study resources abound – you can find many excellent books on the subject.

If you have not tried a more rigorous approach to your Bible study, consider doing so. Join a class that teaches Inductive Bible Study or read one of many books on the topic to help you get started. Reading devotionally is also important, but I think you will enjoy the treasure you are able to unearth by deepening your studies.

THURSDAY – DAY TWENTY-SIX

NANCY GOLDEN

As I have been writing these devotionals and trying to wrap my head around the significance of it all, I am in awe. I can't help but feel the weight of my sinful state that brought Jesus to the cross, but I am also filled with the hope of the Resurrection. Most of all, I feel gratitude for what Jesus has done for all of us. His love for us is incomprehensible to my finite mind – that the Lord of the universe would come to live among us and suffer a horrific death so that we could be cleansed from our sins.

1 Corinthians 6:19-20 tells us, "Do you not know that your bodies are temples of the Holy Spirit, who is in you, whom you have received from God? You are not your own; you were bought at a price. Therefore, honor God with your bodies."

We were bought at a price – We belong to Jesus! Let that soak in. As a follower of Jesus Christ, if you ever find yourself struggling with self-esteem, this is a great reminder of your value: you are priceless! For God so loved the world that He sent His only begotten Son to die for YOU!

~

TODAY'S ACTIVITY: Read John 3:16 with a grateful heart. Start a new habit: when you wake up each morning, before you get out of bed, say out loud, "I belong to Jesus!" and revel in that glorious truth. Feel God's love and peace washing over you. What a wonderful way to start your day!

FRIDAY – DAY TWENTY-SEVEN

NANCY GOLDEN

When an event like Hurricane Harvey in August of 2017 occurs, it catches us completely off guard. We live in such a blessed country of plenty that the devastation wrought by Harvey in Houston was hard to fathom for those of us who were on the outside looking in. But even as far away as Dallas, we saw the effects. Evacuees were making their way into our communities. Most everyone I know was shocked at the gas pump - stations were temporarily running out, and prices started reflecting supply and demand.

For me personally, I watched my son-in-law receive a phone call as we were about to eat Sunday lunch. He didn't stop to eat and was gone within ten minutes, after bringing in schoolbooks and our grandchildren's car seats into the house from his truck. He needed to go directly to pick up two other members of the Army Reserve so they could deploy to Houston with their unit.

Our daughter was now responsible for our three grandchildren by herself, at the beginning of a new school year. They were ready to sacrifice for our neighbors.

Local community organizations and churches stepped up to stand in the gap and serve those who had been devastated by

Harvey. Individuals answered the call for volunteers, and city and government officials worked side by side with citizen volunteers to rescue Harvey victims. Jesus prayed for unity - and in this time of tragedy, it was beautiful to see that prayer being answered over and over.

Instead of looking at each other through the petty lens smeared by our broken humanity full of grievances and complaints, we looked at each other through the same lens Jesus does. All of the divisive issues that had been blasting through the media didn't seem important anymore. We were faced with our common humanity, and how beautiful it was to see our response, the same response that Jesus calls us to - love thy neighbor.

Scripture tells us in John 1:5, "The light shines in the darkness, and the darkness has not overcome it." The Body of Christ continues to shine, and the devastation of Harvey has not overcome us. Help comes from the Lord, and we have the great privilege of being His hands and feet.

During this Lenten season, let us reflect on our common humanity, and the Second Greatest Commandment: God calls us to love our neighbor as ourselves. In the constant climate of social and political divisiveness exacerbated by social media, let us follow Jesus' example and strive for unity.

TODAY'S ACTIVITY: Think about ways you can shine for Christ. Look for a volunteer opportunity in your community. Short-term, long-term, and ongoing needs exist – find one that fits your season of life and commit to helping. Your service to others will glorify your Father in heaven - what a wonderful response to the grace you have received!

SATURDAY – DAY TWENTY-EIGHT

NANCY GOLDEN

E cclesiastes 3:1:

There is a time for everything,
    and a season for every activity under the heavens:

I must have read this verse on my wall around ten million times, but today, for some reason, I focused on the second half. It's quite amazing when you think about it. There is a time to every purpose under heaven. Whatever "time" you are in, be it a job, a family situation, a relationship - happiness, sorrow, contentment, frustration...there is a divine purpose to it. Every purpose under heaven has a God-ordained "time."

Can you see it? Can you trust that God has a purpose for the time you are in, whether it is happy or sad, difficult or easy? Sometimes to fulfill His purposes, He needs to prepare us. Sometimes to fulfill His purposes, He needs to shape our character. Sometimes to fulfill His purposes, He blesses us.

So, when I find myself grumbling about a situation I discover myself in, I can pray for a more heavenly perspective...but I also need to remember to do the same when things are going well and be grateful for God's blessings. Ultimately, no matter what, I need to find peace in knowing that in all things there is indeed a "time" to every purpose under heaven.

TODAY'S ACTIVITY: Take some time to reflect on the different seasons of your life, and how God has worked in each one even in the most difficult of circumstances. Sometimes we can't see it at the time, but we can be confident in the promise of Romans 8:28, that God is working for our good.

In your mind's eye, envision a piece of embroidery and observe the beauty of the image that was so thoughtfully and meticulously sewn. If you are able to hold a real one, you can flip it over and see the chaotic mess of threads and knots that are made on the other side.

God's view is the front – He is working to conform your life into a thing of great beauty. But our view is the back – the messiness of character building, lessons learned, trials endured, and the results of living in a broken world. Be assured that your Heavenly Father is creating a beautiful masterpiece of your life, even when it's hard to see.

SUNDAY – GUEST DEVOTIONAL

DAVID JOSHUA GOLDEN

X αρά (Chara)
χάρις (Charis)
χαίρω (Chairō)

CHARA, the Greek word for Joy used in the New Testament, is one of the heavenly gifts that God promises through His Spirit as mentioned in Galatians 5. This prompts the question: what is Joy? The English dictionary defines it as "pleasure and happiness." This is in line with our modern understanding of Joy, but Chara is something else altogether.

Interestingly, the Greek word for Grace is Charis. Chara and Charis both derive from the same root word, Chairō, which means "to rejoice." God's Joy, distinct from human joy, is intrinsically connected to His Grace. Put simply, it is Grace recognized.

> Though you have not seen him, you love him; and even though you do not see him now, you believe in him and are filled with an inexpressible and glorious joy...
>   -1 Peter 1:8

Belief in Christ and in His Love and Grace for us leads to true Joy. Chara occurs when we acknowledge Grace. It is the direct result of embracing the full measure of God's unmerited favor in our hearts. It's a simple cause and effect: where Grace is welcomed, Joy follows. The words themselves are nearly inter-changeable; they exist together in harmony as divine gifts appointed to us by God and the Holy Spirit.

True Joy can only be found in Christ. It is not the same thing as human joy, which is something that flutters about in response to the wind, never staying for long when life's changing circum-stances interfere with our temporal happiness. Chara Joy is impermeable; it is as resilient and consistent as God Himself, since it is a trait of His character. The gifts Christ promises through the Holy Spirit are completely reliable, surpassing any human emotion.

> So with you: Now is your time of grief, but I will see you again and you will rejoice, and no one will take away your joy.
> - John 16:22

> In the midst of a very severe trial, their overflowing joy and their extreme poverty welled up in rich generosity.
> -2 Corinthians 8:2

Unlike fleeting "pleasure and happiness," Chara is enduring. It doesn't fade or get taken away. It persists, even growing stronger through trials and suffering. God's Joy is complete, abounding—a fulfilling delight that is a byproduct of Grace. Those who walk in Grace experience this Joy, and it will never leave them.

∿

TODAY'S ACTIVITY: How can you walk in Grace today and experience the divine Joy that follows? Take some time to reflect on what God has done for you over the course of your life. Consider not only the gift of salvation, but also the daily, tangible gifts of Grace He provides. Use this time to contemplate the causes for Joy in your life.

Sit down, either by yourself or with someone significant in your life, and compile a list of gifts of Grace you have received. These can be recent or from earlier in your life, significant or small. Maybe it's that job you needed to be able to make ends meet. Perhaps it's a meaningful relationship, or something as simple as a nice walk you've gone on recently. Ultimately, none of us deserve any of these gifts—reflect on them and appreciate the Grace of God that allows us to partake in them.

MONDAY – DAY TWENTY-NINE

NANCY GOLDEN

Lent is a time of reflection and brings an awareness of our mortality. Even when we know those we love are finally out of pain and in the presence of our Savior, saying goodbye is hard. I wish I could pick up the phone and hear my sister's sweet, soothing voice and ready laugh once more.

When I think about my sister Lynn, I think about somebody who was very gifted in the creative arts. I remember from a very young age that she was always doing beautiful drawings. I also remember that she loved to sing and that music was an important part of her life.

But the one thing I remember the most is my sister's love for the Lord and what that looked like in her life. She loved everyone, and she always took younger people under her wing. She had a huge generosity that was displayed in many different ways.

She had a passion for both life and for worshipping the One that gives us life. She had a great deal of enthusiasm for celebrating our family's Jewish roots, which are the roots of Christianity that culminate in Yeshua, our Lord and Savior Jesus Christ.

In the very last text that I received from Lynn, she was thinking of me and not about her own situation. She knew that I love horses and she sent me a picture of two horses. One was blind and eating out of a feed bucket being held up by the other horse, holding it in his teeth so the blind horse could reach it.

She wrote that the picture really touched her and when she saw it she thought of me. Her words were, "This is so beautiful. The blind horse is being helped by a friend." I wrote back, "It is very beautiful! Thank you so much for sharing. Maybe someday I'll write a story about the picture. Love you so much!" Her last text to me was her reply, "Love you so much too!"

I think it resonated with her so much because it was also a picture of who she is. The story I decided to write is her story. My sister would be the horse holding the feed bucket so that the other horse would be able to eat.

I didn't get to live very close to my sister, so I'm not sure of everything she was involved in, but I do know that whatever she devoted herself to, she did it with great enthusiasm. Her legacy is the many people that she invested in with that enthusiasm. I am one of those people, and I am so grateful that my sister was always an encourager to me throughout my life, even when she was journeying through her difficult illness. She was my cheer-leader and one of my best friends. She would hold the feed bucket so that I could eat from it. She was the person who would look around and see what she could do to make someone else's life better.

My sister modeled what it means to be a follower of Jesus Christ. She experienced much joy and did so many things during her lifetime. Lynn was a nurse, an actress, a teacher, and a singer. She was so blessed to have two sons, Danny and Matt. Her husband Brian accompanied her through the trials of this life, of which there were many. She faced each situation with incredible grace, and she persevered, running the race laid out before her with courage and trusting the Lord every step of the way.

Lynn always called me Little Sis, and I called her Big Sis, and I'm very grateful that God gave me such a wonderful big sister for the time I had with her. Somehow, the increased frequency of our phone calls and texts made me feel better because we had some wonderful conversations, more than we have had in years, but also worse, because it makes her absence more profound. It wasn't nearly long enough, but our hearts will always be connected, and someday we will have eternity together. In the meantime, I will follow her beautiful example and do my best to hold the feed bucket for others.

I love you, Big Sis. I sure do miss you. I have the feed bucket ready.

TODAY'S ACTIVITY: Who in your life has been an example or a mentor to you on your Christian walk? Be intentional about expressing your gratitude to them for investing in you. And do your best to commit to holding the feed bucket for others.

TUESDAY – DAY THIRTY

NANCY GOLDEN

Saturday was weird. I work during the week, and usually, I look forward to Saturdays as a day to have an opportunity to sleep a little longer, be a little bit more leisurely, and reach out to family or friends I haven't chatted with lately. While each week is typically filled not only with my day job, but evenings working on promoting my books, I also have lots of other irons in the fire – writing projects I am excited about, learning how to play my ukulele, and riding my bicycle on the greenbelt where we live. Saturdays are usually a welcome respite to do these things. But this Saturday, well...it seemed like the walls were pressing in.

I remember waking up and starting to pray for all of the people I know who are grieving a recent loss, asking God to comfort them. Many of the people on the list had a loved one struck down by COVID-19 or died unexpectedly, all of them gone too soon. I think what finally got to me was the length of the list. I stopped before I got through them all and cried out, "Why, so many, Lord? It's too much to bear." The world has been chaotic for so long. The day seemed unbearable. Peace was elusive.

I never did get my peace that day. But when I woke up Sunday, I made a conscious decision. I needed to do something different. It's okay to have the occasional bad day (and not feel guilty about it) but not to stay there. I didn't sleep in but rather, got up close to my normal workday rise time. We attended church and received the blessing of being with our church family, worshipping God, and receiving an inspiring Word delivered by our pastor. But now what?

Even after church, it felt fairly easy and a little bit tempting to allow myself to slip into the same funk that I was in on Saturday, but I refused. So, what could I do to choose joy instead of despair? This was very uncomfortable for me.

Usually, I don't feel the pangs of depression. Sadness, yes – I am grieving for my sister and for dear friends who have gone to Heaven. I miss them!! But I can usually turn my thoughts to the happy memories I have of them and not stay sad too long – there is so much to be done, and I know they wouldn't want me to over-extend my grief to a point that it interferes with daily life. I didn't know what to do...

So, I did something different. Usually, I am stuck inside at my computer. Usually, we eat inside. Usually, I have an agenda that I follow so that I can get done what I need to. I have a Post-it note list of "to-dos" for the day. But instead – I moved my day outside into our backyard. I cleaned off our patio table and set my computer up on it.

I stayed outside ALL day. We ate outside. I read my book outside. I worked on my latest novel outside. And in between, I played ping pong with my husband, played soccer with my dog, and threw a frisbee. I grabbed my ukulele and practiced the chords I had been trying to learn. I laughed. I read the scriptures in our prayer garden. I watched the birds. I sang spontaneously. I reflected on how blessed we are. I didn't finish my Post-it note list, but I found peace.

Sometimes, peace is elusive. The trials of this world can be very hard to bear. If you find yourself pressed down, perhaps it's time to do something different. Even a little different, like hanging out in your backyard (or a park if you don't have a back-yard). Or grab a ukulele and play a few chords...

My wish is for you to allow yourself to be human and grieve when your heart hurts – but don't stay there too long. There is still much beauty around us, even in despair. God is still working on our behalf – even when it is hard to see, and He grieves with us.

One last image comes to mind as I write this. A picture of light even in the darkness – a video I watched of playful guards at the Ukraine-Slovakia border helping refugee families with their belongings and the infectious laughter of the children as they spread joy even in desperate circumstances.

There is always light, and it will overcome.

TODAY'S ACTIVITY: Part of our Lenten journey is acknowledging that we live in a broken world. But we should never forget the hope we have in Jesus – Matthew 5:14-16 tells us:

> You are the light of the world. A town built on a hill cannot be hidden. Neither do people light a lamp and put it under a bowl. Instead, they put it on its stand, and it gives light to everyone in the house. In the same way, let your light shine before others, that they may see your good deeds and glorify your Father in heaven.

Let your light shine today. How can you be like those guards and be intentional about bringing someone else joy in difficult circumstances? It can be as simple as reaching out to someone who has recently experienced a loss. Invite them to lunch or bring them a plate of cookies. Show them they are not alone in the world – simple actions can bring great comfort.

WEDNESDAY – DAY THIRTY-ONE

NANCY GOLDEN

We live in such tension as Christians in the world today. I heard one person call it living "in-between." We are citizens of Heaven longing for Jesus to return as we struggle to make sense of a broken world. We must remember that as the body of Christ, when one rejoices, we also rejoice, and when one suffers, we suffer with them.

We must also remember that we are called to bring light to the darkness. Let us pray for one another, encourage each other, and bear one another's burdens. Share the Gospel with a world that, like all of us, desperately needs a Savior.

It's pretty simple, really. Love the Lord your God with all your heart, soul, mind, and strength. Love your neighbor as yourself. Wouldn't it be a wonderful world if we all did that? It will be someday when Christ returns... in the meantime, we need to keep our eyes focused on God and reflect His love to those around us. Not just during Lent, but all year long.

While it is frustrating to see so much pain and suffering in the world, we have an advantage - we know how the story ends! We might have to walk through some very difficult situations in our lives, but what a blessing to know that we will never walk through them alone.

Do you know someone without hope in Christ? The greatest act of love you can do is to share with them the hope that you have. It all begins by simply spending time with them and loving them, and opportunities will arise naturally. Don't wait. You never know what tomorrow may bring.

TODAY'S ACTIVITY: Think about those within your sphere of influence who don't know Christ. Commit to praying for them and ask the Holy Spirit to provide opportunities to share your faith. Be prepared to reflect the love of your Savior, so the Holy Spirit can work in their lives through you. What an honor and a privilege to point others to Jesus!!

THURSDAY – DAY THIRTY-TWO

NANCY GOLDEN

In today's world, it is easy to find ourselves overwhelmed with busyness. The pressures of school activities, stressful workdays, ministry opportunities, family visits and caregiving, shopping, church activities, and attending school and church functions can make the days pass in a blur. You may also find your mailbox filled daily with solicitations for donations to various worthy causes. It can be enough for you to want to pack your bags and escape the incessant responsibilities that demand so much of your time! That is where the example of our Lord Jesus comes in.

Luke 5:16 tells us, "But Jesus often withdrew to lonely places and prayed." All through Scripture, Jesus takes time away from people to spend time with His Father. He understood the importance of both praying for—and with—others, but He also understood the importance of being alone with God.

Jesus spent forty days in the wilderness in preparation for His earthly ministry. He often left the crowds He was preaching to and went up the mountainside to pray alone. He sometimes went to a garden in the quiet of the evening for prayer.

Jesus ministered to many during His earthly ministry, but He did so according to His Father's will, and He constantly spent time with God. What a great example for us during this Lenten season! You are not called to participate in every activity or event, and you don't have to help everywhere. Quiet your heart and see where God is leading. Don't forget to spend time with Him.

Jesus had many purposes during His time on Earth, and His greatest purpose is found in Matthew 1:21, to save us from our sins, but He is also an example for us, as to how we can live a life pleasing to God.

Seek God's will in all that you do and spend time with Him. Psalm 46:10 reads, "Be still, and know that I am God." Perhaps you need to take a pause from the whirlwind of activities around you and let your Lord minister to your soul.

TODAY'S ACTIVITY: We rush through our days trying to get all of our stuff done, and items on our "to-do" list checked off, but when we look back, it's not the problems we solved and tasks we completed that we will remember - it is the experiences of love and laughter, ministry and healing, giving and receiving help, and the sharing of joys and sorrows, that will have given our days true meaning. Life with God is a journey as well as a destination. Enjoy the journey!

Matthew 6:33 tells us, "But seek first his kingdom and his righteousness, and all these things will be given to you as well."

Examine your life and see what changes you may need to make in your daily routine so that you can seek God first and enjoy the journey. Allow yourself to be open to new possibilities while discarding old habits that wear you out but don't have eternal value.

FRIDAY – DAY THIRTY-THREE

NANCY GOLDEN

Lent is a season about God's forgiveness – and a reminder that we should forgive one another. I have been thinking about forgiveness a lot lately. Many people struggle with it, either unable to forgive themselves for something they have done or unable to forgive someone else for hurting them.

When I think about God's limitless grace and that it is through Christ's sacrifice at the cross that we have received forgiveness for all of our transgressions – what's even more amazing is that God initiated it! We read in Romans 5:8, "But God demonstrates his own love for us in this: While we were still sinners, Christ died for us."

He died for us, knowing we were a mess, yet loving us anyway. His forgiveness heals us, and if we are unable to forgive ourselves or others, we are unable to fully experience the peace that comes from the healing power of Christ.

When we forgive others, we choose to follow the example Christ set for us. I believe God uses that step of faith to release healing not only in the person offering forgiveness and the person being forgiven but also in anyone else affected by the broken relationship.

It's no wonder we sometimes wrestle with forgiveness. Forgiveness is a universal struggle, which is why songs are written about it. Forgiving oneself may be hardest of all. For those battling events from the past, it might help to remember what Paul writes in Philippians 3:12-14:

> Not that I have already obtained all this, or have already arrived at my goal, but I press on to take hold of that for which Christ Jesus took hold of me. Brothers and sisters, I do not consider myself yet to have taken hold of it. But one thing I do: Forgetting what is behind and straining toward what is ahead, I press on toward the goal to win the prize for which God has called me heavenward in Christ Jesus.

Many people focus on verse 14, but notice what Paul says in verse 13: "Forgetting what is behind" is so important. We need to NOT allow our past to dictate our present or influence our future. It doesn't mean we won't have consequences from the past that we will have to deal with, but the past need NOT affect the choices we make today or determine what is yet to come.

If you consider Paul's past before he became a Christian, he crossed many lines in persecuting the church. This becomes very powerful because he puts his transgressions behind him, and by focusing on what lies ahead, he overcomes his past to become a great pillar of the church whose influence through the Holy Spirit has guided Christians for thousands of years. Wow!

Paul initially had to deal with a lot of unpleasantness because of what he had done previously, but he didn't let that stop him – something you might want to share to encourage someone who may be struggling with their past. Paul's example reassures us that there are no lost causes and that we can all have a new beginning. God forgives us when we ask; therefore, we should be able to forgive ourselves and receive the peace and hope that comes with the grace He freely offers.

For those of us who have trouble forgiving others, I don't believe you will ever be truly at peace until you do. It doesn't even matter how the other person responds (if they are even around to respond). Offering forgiveness is an intentional action that flows out of your heart. While it is hoped that it blesses the person you are forgiving, their positive response is not a requirement.

I believe God gives us a great gift by teaching us to forgive one another, and it is also for our own benefit – a heart weighed down by the bitterness of being unforgiving can never experience true joy.

TODAY'S ACTIVITY: Scripture is clear on God's desire for us to forgive one another. Paul writes in Ephesians 4:32, "Be kind and compassionate to one another, forgiving each other, just as in Christ God forgave you."

If you have something weighing you down, pray about taking the steps God may be calling you to take, so that restoration can occur through the power of Jesus Christ and despair and disappointment can be replaced with healing and love.

SATURDAY – DAY THIRTY-FOUR

NANCY GOLDEN

While this is a season that turns our thoughts towards our own mortality, it is astonishing to think that the God of the universe, the King of kings and Lord of lords, chose to experience death on our behalf. Jesus came to Earth on a mission—fully man and fully God. When we recognize that He left the heavens knowing He was destined to die, we should be filled with amazement. His love brought Him here, and He drank the cup set before Him to its very last dregs—dying an excruciating death upon the cross because of that love.

Our Savior is not a distant God unable to understand what we feel. He left His heavenly home and walked among us. He was anguished in the garden and knew what was coming, yet He stayed because of His incomprehensible love for us. How beautiful it is that we have a mediator who fully understands what it is to be human. He felt all of our human emotions, yet He was without sin (Hebrews 4:15). While perfect, He took on our sin in a perfect atoning sacrifice to take away the sins of the world.

Let us turn our thoughts to the incredible sacrifice of our Lord and remember that He was one of us. Death of our bodies awaits us, for to dust they will return. But as we solemnly consider that our earthly bodies will one day perish, we can take great hope in the fact that our soul never dies. Through Jesus dying on the cross, if we confess with our mouth that Jesus is Lord and believe that God raised Him from the dead (Romans 10:9), we will also join Him in the Resurrection, and spend eternity with Him—Hallelujah!

~

TODAY'S ACTIVITY: Reflect on Hebrews 4:15, "For we do not have a high priest who is unable to empathize with our weaknesses, but we have one who has been tempted in every way, just as we are—yet he did not sin."

Let us bring all our emotions, including our fears, to our Savior. He understands us for He once was one of us.

Consider Ephesians 2:8-9, "For it is by grace you have been saved, through faith—and this is not from yourselves, it is the gift of God—not by works, so that no one can boast."

Have you taken that step of faith? While this is a season of repentance for the Christian, it is also one of hope. We have a Savior who has fully atoned for our sins, so despite our sinful state, we have the hope of eternity—but only if we choose to put our faith in Him.

If you are reading this and have not accepted Jesus as your Lord and Savior, I pray you choose to do so (and find a local church to answer any of your questions and enter into a community of faith with other Christians). And if you have already, fall to your knees in gratitude for what He has done for you!

PALM SUNDAY

NANCY GOLDEN

Today is Palm Sunday, the beginning of Holy Week recognized by those who are followers of Jesus Christ. As excited as we all get about Christmas (the birth of our Savior) it runs second to the most exciting holiday of all in the Christian calendar.

In the secular world that holiday is known as Easter Sunday but to understand the meaning of Easter in all its glory—Christians refer to it as Resurrection Day—the day that Jesus conquered death after bearing incredible torture on our behalf —and all of this driven by His love for us!

The Bible tells us in Romans 10:9-10,

> if you confess with your mouth that Jesus is Lord and believe in your heart that God raised him from the dead, you will be saved. For with the heart one believes and is justified, and with the mouth one confesses and is saved.

Easter commemorates God raising Jesus from the dead, but Jesus had to endure horrific agony on our behalf to get there.

Palm Sunday is the day Jesus arrived in Jerusalem—knowing what was ahead, yet still choosing to do so.

Often referred to as the Triumphal Entry, the humble arrival of Jesus riding upon a donkey fulfilled Old Testament prophecy (Zechariah 9:9) about the coming of the Messiah. Crowds lined the road, waving palm branches in homage to Him and shouting, "Hosanna to the Son of David! Blessed is He who comes in the name of the Lord," in recognition that Jesus was the anointed One of Israel.

AND SO IT STARTED...

WE LIVE in tremendous tension as the world remains in a constant state of chaos and uncertainty, and there seems to be no end in sight. It is good to remember God's purpose through His Son Jesus Christ for humanity even when the unfathomable happens.

JOHN 3:16 SAYS,

> For God so loved the world that he gave his one and only Son, that whoever believes in him shall not perish but have eternal life.

We have a hope that is enduring, a Lord who loves us, and a purpose ordained by Him for our time on Earth.

Holy Week is a special reminder that God's love for us is relentless, incomprehensible, sacrificial, and unconditional. Perfect and without sin, yet willing to die for us – that is God's amazing love!

TODAY'S ACTIVITY: Think about the times you may have been impressed by a leader with the rich trappings of their position. Now, think about how Jesus chose to proclaim His kingship. Note how Jesus turns all of our thinking upside down.

The kingdom of God is not found in material wealth, but in a humble servant's heart. How should that impact how we live our lives? Reflect on any changes you may feel led to make in how you view the world, in light of the example our Savior gave us.

MONDAY – DAY THIRTY-FIVE

Yesterday, we celebrated Palm Sunday and being a horsewoman, I wanted to share a fun fact about Jesus' triumphal ride. Jesus rode into Jerusalem to publicly proclaim He is the Messiah and King of Israel, fulfilling the Old Testament prophecy found in Zechariah 9:9. We read in Matthew 21:1-11,

> As they approached Jerusalem and came to Bethphage on the Mount of Olives, Jesus sent two disciples, saying to them, "Go to the village ahead of you, and at once you will find a donkey tied there, with her colt by her. Untie them and bring them to me. If anyone says anything to you, say that the Lord needs them, and he will send them right away."
>
> This took place to fulfill what was spoken through the prophet:
> "Say to Daughter Zion,
> 'See, your king comes to you,
> gentle and riding on a donkey,
> and on a colt, the foal of a donkey.'"
> The disciples went and did as Jesus had instructed them.

They brought the donkey and the colt and placed their cloaks on them for Jesus to sit on. A very large crowd spread their cloaks on the road, while others cut branches from the trees and spread them on the road. The crowds that went ahead of him and those that followed shouted,

"Hosanna to the Son of David!"

"Blessed is he who comes in the name of the Lord!"

"Hosanna in the highest heaven!"

When Jesus entered Jerusalem, the whole city was stirred and asked, "Who is this?"

The crowds answered, "This is Jesus, the prophet from Nazareth in Galilee."

While this is a wonderful account of the triumphal entry of Jesus into Jerusalem, to those of us familiar with horses, it is also a miracle and shows that all of creation recognizes Jesus as the Son of God. Let me explain.

Jesus was riding the foal of a donkey – a young, unbroken equine that had not been trained to be ridden. Further, all equines are prey animals on high alert; they must be trained to accept anything on their back, and a cloak waving around them would send any uninitiated equine into a panic.

The fact that the disciples were able to place their cloaks on the donkey without it fleeing speaks to an incredible peace that can only be explained by Jesus' presence. Next, Jesus mounts this untrained donkey – yet no Wild West Show occurs. The donkey accepts his rider with no fuss, and then proceeds to what was essentially a parade – people lining the road waving palm leaves and shouting.

We typically spend days, if not weeks, training our horses not to spook during parades. As prey animals, they are wired to run at the sight of anything they think may cause them harm.

Waving palms and the unexpected noises that come from a

crowd would be enough to try the nerves of the most seasoned of equines. Yet this young donkey carried the Lord of the universe without fuss, bringing Him safely into Jerusalem.

How wonderful that Jesus chose to come humbly in His triumphal entry, much like He did when He came to Earth by being born in a manger, accessible to all. The animals of the manger and the foal of the donkey carrying Him into Jerusalem knew who He was and worshipped Him.

Finally, one more interesting fact about our story. Take a look at the back of a donkey when you get an opportunity. You will see a line that follows his back, and another line that intersects it at his withers. The animal that bore Jesus into Jerusalem during His triumphal entry bears the symbol of the cross on his back! How precious that this humble equine carries the symbol of what Jesus did for us.

TODAY'S ACTIVITY: Revelation 5:13,

> Then I heard every creature in heaven and on earth and under
> the earth and on the sea, and all that is in them, saying:
>> "To him who sits on the throne and to the Lamb
>> be praise and honor and glory and power,
>> for ever and ever!"

Think about the scope of God's love, that all of creation is made by Him and for Him. Let that color your perception when viewing the living creatures around you. Marvel that each one has a special place in His creation, ordained by God, and living according to His design.

TUESDAY – DAY THIRTY-SIX

As we continue our journey towards Easter Sunday, focusing on the sacrifice of our Lord and Savior, it is good to remember to not only keep Jesus in Easter but also to invite Him into our lives throughout the year. Jesus came down from Heaven to save us from our sins. When we call out to Him, we receive not only eternal salvation but also His peace here on Earth.

Putting Christ at the center of our lives changes everything. Gaining the eternal perspective of Heaven helps us walk in this world, with all its pain and suffering, and enables us to do so with joy. The joy we have in Christ overflows into our relationships and our daily lives, touching others even as it touches us.

God's love for us is beautiful, extravagant, and unforgettable. Each one of us has a purpose under Heaven, and we are each given a season to live it out. Our ultimate objective is to love God and to love others. That looks different for each one of us because we are all unique, but the end result is the same: In whatever we do, let us honor God and seek to please Him, and love one another in both our words and actions. Life here on

Earth is both precious and short. Let's be an expression of God's love for one another each and every day.

TODAY'S ACTIVITY: Look around you. Is there an elderly neighbor or perhaps a lonely teenager living near you? What can you do today to love and encourage them? How can you become more intentional about loving the people around you? Write down the names God brings to your mind and commit to reaching out to them more frequently.

WEDNESDAY – DAY THIRTY-SEVEN

L ent is a great time to reflect on how God has been working in your life and to thank Him for everything He has done. For today's devotional, I am sharing a love letter I wrote to God.

Dear Heavenly Father,

Lying awake in bed this morning, my mind turned to all of the blessings You have poured upon me throughout my life. My heart filled with gratitude, and I wanted to thank You for Your everlasting love, mercy, and compassion. You know I got it wrong a lot, did things that I am ashamed to admit, and had many selfish moments, yet You continue to love me despite myself. I have walked some pretty tough roads in life, yet I always knew You were right there with me, and You carried me when I couldn't carry myself. You wept when I wept and You wrapped me in Your peace and love during my worst moments.

You never stopped planning for my good, even when I couldn't see it in my current circumstances. I look back at the poor decisions I made and You, in Your great love for me, redeemed each one. I am grateful that You know I am frail and weak and that You look into my heart to know my true intentions, especially when I give in to the temptations of this world and fail You. You don't give up on me and You forgive me. You even help me forgive myself.

I also looked back on all of the people You have brought into my life. The gift of my husband Phil, my son Josh and most recently, his beautiful wife Naomi. My sisters and brothers and sisters-in-law. The daughters you brought into my life, not by blood, but from love. The countless people from around the world that have blessed us with their friendship.

The experiences You have blessed me with over the years are innumerable and when I start reflecting on all of the opportunities You have provided me, I am so grateful and humbled. Ephesians 3:20 comes to mind. I have been able to do more than I could have ever thought of or imagined for myself. I would list them here, but I am afraid it would look like I am being pretentious because You are so extravagant in Your generosity – truly, each one has been possible because of You.

The list is long and contains accomplishments I personally desired because You are a God that loves us and sings over us as we fulfill what You have created us to love – such as riding a horse that has never been ridden before or becoming an author. You also exult over us as we strive to further Your Kingdom using the gifts you have blessed us with – such as teaching and participating in community outreach.

My son reminded me of something else today – You give us so many small miracles to be thankful for. Sometimes we lose sight of that because we are hoping for the bigger ones, but in all things, You are moving Your plans forward and blessing us along the way. And when our hearts cry out to You because we can't feel You near – you make the leaves dance where there is no wind (Thank you, Father – I will never forget that day!).

Thank you for Your amazing love for us and for the incredible gift of eternal life we have through Your Son, Jesus Christ. I can never thank you enough. Please help me to be a reflection of Your love to the world.

Love Always,
  Your Child,

Nancy

TODAY'S ACTIVITY: I signed it "Child" because we are His children! 1 John 1:3 tells us, "See what great love the Father has lavished on us, that we should be called children of God! And that is what we are!"

We live in a broken world. Suffering is all around us. But there is also beauty if we have eyes to see. We can be a part of that beauty by loving one another, despite our differences.

Take time to write your own love letter to God. As a thank you to Him who loves us beyond measure, see what you can do to be a light in the darkness.

THURSDAY – DAY THIRTY-EIGHT

"That's not fair! He got a bigger bonus. She gets to drive a company car, and I don't. He got hired instead of me. She got an A and never showed up to class..." How many times have you caught yourself saying things like that? I have, more times than I would like to admit. But when I do, my husband Phil has some extraordinary wisdom to share. He always says, "Be thankful that God is not fair with us."

Instead of being offended or upset because something didn't go our way - remember that in the most important thing of all, God is not fair - and thank God He chose not to be! Instead of allowing us to reap the consequences of our sin - God sent His Son to take our place, so that we could have eternal life with Him.

That wasn't fair to God's Son, yet Jesus did it for us because He loves us. It makes you think twice before getting upset when things don't go your way—doesn't it? Thank You, God, for loving us so much that You chose to be unfair. Thank You for Your grace!

Today is a special day in the Christian liturgical calendar, Maundy Thursday, the Last Supper Jesus had with His disciples as recorded in the Gospels. It is this day that Christ portrayed the ultimate picture of humble service before presiding over the Passover meal when He instituted the biblical basis for the practice of communion. He who was without sin kneeled and lovingly bathed the dirt from the feet of His disciples, setting an example of how we should be toward one another.

Let's follow the example of our Lord and try to cultivate hearts that are happy for others when they receive blessings rather than being jealous, indignant, or offended. Let us love one another with the sacrificial, humble love of our Savior.

TODAY'S ACTIVITY: I teach at Dallas Christian College, and occasionally, I feel led to extend a deadline for a paper, even after some of my students have turned theirs in on time. Some of my students become angry since they had worked hard and did what the assignment required. They become upset when I offer their classmates—who have not finished in time—grace.

That is when I have them read Matthew 20:1-16. Read this passage of Scripture. What does this parable teach us about what our attitudes should be when someone else receives a blessing?

FRIDAY – DAY THIRTY-NINE

W hen someone is at the brink of death, their last words often revolve around what they hold to be most important, revealing their deepest concerns. Even in dying, we can see that for Jesus, His greatest concern was for us, rather than the excruciating pain that He was bearing. His desire to articulate His thoughts from the cross must have brought shockwaves of pain as He struggled to lift His torn body upward against the nails, to draw enough breath to speak.

Russell Bradley Jones writes in his powerful little book, Gold from Golgotha (Moody Books ©1945),

> Everything at Calvary is significant, but in a very special sense,
> the Savior's seven words, spoken from the heart of His vicar-
> ious suffering, interpret Him to mankind.

Scripture records that Jesus spoke seven times. Let's take the next two days to examine more closely these words He deemed so important, He uttered them from the cross in the midst of His passion.

Luke 23:34, Jesus said, "Father, forgive them, for they do not know what they are doing."

Amidst great suffering, Jesus thought of others, not Himself. He came for the lost, and in this prayer, He was asking His Father to give them a chance for redemption rather than the judgment they deserved. He asked God to allow them a chance to believe. We can interpret "Jesus said" to mean "Jesus kept saying." In the original Greek, the verb is imperfect, indicating repeating action in past time. Jesus' prayer was a continuous petition on our behalf in the midst of His suffering.

Luke 23:39-43, "One of the criminals who hung there hurled insults at him: 'Aren't you the Messiah? Save yourself and us!' But the other criminal rebuked him. 'Don't you fear God,' he said, 'since you are under the same sentence? We are punished justly, for we are getting what our deeds deserve. But this man has done nothing wrong.' Then he said, 'Jesus, remember me when you come into your kingdom.' Jesus answered him, 'Truly I tell you, today you will be with me in paradise .'"

Jesus faced temptation just as He did in the wilderness and in the Garden of Gethsemane. One thief asked for physical release, challenging Jesus to show His power and save them if He really was the Messiah. The other thief appealed to Jesus to "Remember me when you come into your kingdom." He wasn't asking for release from his cross but from his sin. What is amazing is the choice before Jesus – the cessation of torture or the prize of His agony: totally unworthy sinners such as the self-confessed criminal hanging next to Him – and each one of us!

John 19:26-27, "When Jesus saw his mother there, and the disciple whom he loved standing nearby, he said to her,

'Woman, here is your son,' and to the disciple, 'Here is your mother.' From that time on, this disciple took her into his home."

Notice, Jesus addressed Mary as "woman" instead of "mother." He assigned John as His substitute and, in those words, severed His earthly relationship with Mary. She was now free to have the higher relationship of believer, with Jesus as her Savior. Heartbreaking as it must have been for both of them, it was necessary for Mary to lose her son in order for all of us to gain our salvation. It is hard to even begin to fathom that kind of sacrificial love.

TODAY'S ACTIVITY: While today's devotional is difficult to read, it is an amazing picture of the love Jesus has for us. Spend some quiet time with God today, making sure to thank Jesus for the depth of His love that led Him to the cross on our behalf.

If you are able to find a local church offering it, attend a Tenebrae service. It is a deeply moving experience that will walk you through the Scriptures pertaining to Good Friday and our Lord's incredible sacrifice.

SATURDAY – DAY FORTY

Yesterday, we examined the first three sayings of Jesus as He hung on the cross. Today, let's continue our journey by reflecting on the final four sayings uttered by our Lord before He drew His last breath.

> Matthew 27:46, At about the ninth hour, Jesus cried out in a loud voice, "Eloi, Eloi, lema sabachthani?" which means, "My God, my God, why have you forsaken me?"

2 Corinthians 5:21 informs us, "God made him who had no sin to be sin for us, so that in him we might become the righteousness of God." On the cross, bearing our sins in the depths of agony, Jesus' soul cries out as He descends into hell for us – His Father is no longer there.

In this terrible time of forsakenness, we see the evidence of God's wrath toward sin. Because Jesus was assuming the sin of the world, and God is holy and cannot be in its proximity, removing His presence from His beloved Son was imperative. Having never been separated before - we cannot fathom the pain that must have been felt by both. This speaks to the incomprehensible sacrifice of both the Father and the Son—all for the sake of love.

> John 19:28, Later, knowing that all was now completed, Jesus said, "I am thirsty."

Jesus said, "I am thirsty" after "all was now completed." What He set out to do at the cross was complete. There was nothing more to be done. Jesus was also fulfilling prophecy and identifying Himself as the Messiah in those three simple words. In Psalm 69, His suffering is predicted, as well as His thirst when He would be offered vinegar to drink.

> John 19:30, After receiving the drink, Jesus said, "It is finished." He then bowed His head and gave up His spirit.

In the original Greek, "it is finished" may be translated as one word – "tetelestai" –meaning "It was finished and as a result it is forever done." There is nothing left to be done to complete the work that the Lord Jesus Christ perfected at the cross. "It" is the suffering of the full punishment of all guilt for all time. He paid the penalty due for sin with His perfect sacrifice. Sinners can now approach God through their faith in Jesus and because of His righteousness. A place in Heaven is now possible because God's divine justice has been satisfied. Nothing more is needed. All that is left to be done by us is to accept Jesus as Lord and receive the gift of His grace.

> Luke 23:46, Jesus called out, "Father, into your hands I commit my spirit." With that, He breathed His last.

The last words of Jesus show His death was voluntary, that He chose to give up His life for us. In His final words, He is the

Victorious Son, committing His all to His Father. His sacrifice is the best example for us—a voluntary commitment of ourselves into the hands of God with all that we are and have.

We can't understand everything that Christ said in His final hours, but there is much that we can and should study and reflect on. In Russell Bradley Jones's words from his book, Gold from Golgotha (Moody Books ©1945),

> Golgotha is the place where the contrast between the Savior's heart of grace and man's heart of rebellion is most striking. Golgotha is the focal point of revelation and history and experience. There God did His best and man did his worst. There faith is justified, hope assured, and love conquers.

TODAY'S ACTIVITY: We end today feeling emotionally wrung out. No words can express what we have witnessed, all for the sake of love. Jesus chose the cross so that we could be with Him – His whole purpose for coming to Earth culminating in His excruciating death, but wait!

Thank God, as Christians, we know how the story ends. Hold on, Easter people – the Resurrection is coming! Invite someone that does not know the story to go with you to an Easter service and share the best news of all!

EASTER SUNDAY

NANCY GOLDEN

Imagine yourself having made the trip to Jerusalem for the Festival of the Passover with such joy. You look forward to going every year. It is a wonderful opportunity for you to be obedient to the Lord by celebrating the Passover meal, and what better place to do so than in Jerusalem, the religious capital of your faith? You also get to see old friends while making new ones. Your cousin lives in the city, so you even have a place to stay.

It isn't that far from your village called Emmaus – roughly 7 ½ miles. You look forward to the two-and-a-half-hour walk, especially because you'll have the company of Cleopas, who closes his blacksmith shop every year to attend. You both had met Jesus of Nazareth and had become his followers. You had heard he would be there, but you had never imagined the horror you would experience that Friday. The events happened so quickly that it was almost incomprehensible.

You find yourself standing by a cross, watching as Jesus is crucified. He hangs on that cross for hours, until He finally gives up His spirit and breathes His last. The sky turns dark, mourning with you. The ground shakes under your feet as if the very earth protests His death.

You can scarcely breathe as you watch Jesus being brought down and placed in a tomb. You return to your cousin's home, exhausted and weighted with a terrible sadness. You will be heading home on the first day of the week, but right now, all you can do is cling to your family and try to comprehend what has happened.

Heartbroken for Jesus and His family and uncertain of what it means for the future, you are further shocked on the third day since the crucifixion when you are preparing to head back to your village and hear the news that Jesus' body is missing from the tomb. All of this is too much to bear. You just want to get home and get as distant from the terrible events of the last few days as possible.

You and Cleopas start your journey back to your village. The flower-filled fields, green pastures, and singing birds are incongruent with your mood. You had been so excited that Jesus would be the Redeemer of Israel, and now all of your hopes are dashed.

Walking the dusty road, you and Cleopas can't help but talk about everything that happened. Rather than helping, it makes you both even more downcast. Jesus was a prophet, powerful in word and deed, before God and all of the people. You really thought He would be Israel's salvation. And now He was not only dead, His tomb had been desecrated – He was inexplicably gone.

As you and Cleopas continue to discuss these events and its implications, a man you don't recognize approaches and begins to walk alongside you. He asks you what you are talking about, and you explain to him what has happened in Jerusalem in the past few days. Much to your surprise, he replies with an admonition about Jesus having to suffer before entering His glory.

You aren't sure what he means, but he keeps talking, and you find yourself riveted as he explains the Scriptures to you regarding Jesus, starting from Moses, accompanying you and Cleopas as you walk the dusty road. You feel a strange sensation in your chest. A comforting warmth burns in your heart. You briefly wonder what his name is, but you don't want to interrupt him. The time flies by, and you arrive at your village.

The man begins to say farewell, but it is late, and you have never felt this way before. "Please, stay," you find yourself blurting out. There is something about the man you can't explain, and you don't want your time with him to end.

He turns his gaze fully upon you, and you are startled by the depth of love and compassion you find there. "I will stay with you," he replies. For some reason, you can't explain, your heart feels even more full. You feel complete.

You enter your home and immediately begin preparations for dinner. You lay some bread made from parched grain upon the table along with some fruit and cheese, apologizing for the simple meal, but it is getting late, and everyone is hungry.

The man merely smiles at your words and reaches for the bread. He takes it into his hands, gives thanks, and breaks it. As he hands a piece of it to you, you realize who the man is breaking bread at your table – it is Jesus!

Before you can utter a word, he turns his gaze upon you once again, and your heart leaps in your chest. You have never in all of your life felt such intense joy. A gentle smile crosses his countenance, and then, much to your astonishment, he disappears in front of your eyes.

You look at Cleopas, pressing your hand against your chest. A sense of profound hope and peace envelops your entire being. The Son of God—resurrected from the dead—had walked with you back to Emmaus and sat at your table. He did just as the Scriptures he explained said he would. He is risen!

TODAY'S ACTIVITY: Today's devotional comes from the events recorded in Luke 24:13- 35, often referred to as On the Road to Emmaus. When we talk about the Resurrection, we typically do so from a distance – describing the events that unfold around it. Today, our goal is to make it more personal.

Read today's devotional again a second time. Take your time and allow yourself to explore the feelings you have in response to each event being described. Move through the devotional as if you are truly there. Feel your heart burning within you at His words. When you come to the last sentence, feel the joy that those words evoke.

As followers of Jesus Christ, we have traveled through the desert of Lent to our final destination – the joy of the Resurrection and the hope we have in Him for eternal life! Hallelujah!

THE COLORS OF LENT

LAURA FRITZ

L ent is a 40-day period between Ash Wednesday and
Easter, a time when we reflect on what our Lord did for
us on the cross. Visual cues that can aid us during this
time of contemplation are all around us. Reflecting on colors
during Lent can be incredibly impactful. There is no one official
designation for the meaning of the colors of Lent, or even which
colors should be included. Different faith traditions have their
own definitions, and that can even vary within the tradition. The
important thing to note is that the colors can serve as visual
reminders of spiritual truths, so let them speak to your heart as
you move through this special season.

Purple is a prevalent color we see during Lent. With over 40
references to it in the Bible, purple was elevated as an important
color in biblical times. The Old Testament points to this significance, as purple was one of the four colors God commanded be
used for the Tabernacle curtains made of the finest linens. It is
often a symbol of royalty. When the Roman soldiers mocked
Jesus before His crucifixion, they dressed Him in a purple robe,
yelling, "Hail, king of the Jews!".

The royal symbolism goes back to ancient times when only

the wealthy could afford purple linens. They didn't have the luxury of chemical dyes as we do today. It is said that purple was extracted from cerulean mussels which were very expensive to obtain.

Imagine the incredible celebration that would have occurred during that time if someone paid the high cost and handed out purple linens to everyone in their community, regardless of their status. Purple can be a reminder to celebrate how our access to the true King of kings isn't dependent on our wealth or nobility. Our gift of salvation came at a cost much higher than extracting purple from cerulean mussels. Jesus paid this price for ALL of us when He suffered and died a brutal death on the cross. Purple is a powerful reminder to celebrate this gift.

White is another color that speaks to me during this time of year. I love the beauty of white lilies on the table at Easter brunch as they represent the bright light, joy, and triumph of Jesus' resurrection. Because this only happens through the blood of Jesus Christ, the color red also has a significant meaning during Lent. It is a reminder of the atoning sacrifice of Jesus on the cross. The Bible reminds us that the blood of Jesus makes us white as snow. Without the shedding of blood, there is no forgiveness of sin.

Perhaps there is another reminder we can draw from the color red, which is often associated with a stop sign. Red can be an encouragement to stop and pause for reflection during these 40 days of Lent. If we don't pause long enough, the white lily may mean nothing more than a beautiful flower we see on a table set for brunch. We'll miss the opportunity to reflect on what the color symbolizes.

In addition to noticing the colors already in our paths, we can also be intentional and creative by adding these colors into our lives during Lent. For example, lighting a purple candle at home may remind you of the high price Jesus paid to make salvation accessible to all who call upon Him as Lord and Savior. Arranging a bouquet of red and white tulips can remind us of how God's blood was necessary for the glorious Resurrection. It can be as simple as writing in a journal with colored pens. Don't miss the opportunity to reflect on the colors of Lent this season.

BENEDICTION

May you move through each day with repentance and reflection, yet filled with the hope of the Resurrection and the joy of experiencing God's mercy and graciousness! Live in the blessed assurance of salvation Jesus provides to those who call upon Him as Lord and Savior. Be a light in the darkness, love one another, and be forgiving of one another as Christ forgives us. Go in peace.

TAKING BACK THE GOSPEL
COMING MAY 2024

The Second Greatest Commandment (Matthew 22:36-40) tells us to love our neighbors as ourselves, and The Great Commission (Matthew 28:16-20) tells us to go and make disciples. By combining these two commandments from our Lord, we are able to share our faith with those around us in a natural way.

In the pages of this book, you'll find ways that you can share the Gospel that are both comfortable for you and effective. Since it is all about sharing the love of Christ by building relationships with those around you and allowing the Holy Spirit to work through you – the pressure is off! God will use you in the ways that He has gifted you, and when we understand that it is our job to be obedient, but the end results are His, we are free to focus on building relationships rather than trying to follow a preplanned agenda.

You will learn about why you should evangelize and how to go about it, with plenty of examples and encouragement along the way. You won't find a huge, scholarly tome here – but an easy-to-read book that is intentionally not very long. We think you will find it very convenient to fit this study into even the busiest of schedules, and still gain the tools you need to approach evangelism with joy and confidence.

Nine chapters lend themselves well to a nine-week group study, but they can also be read individually at a more rapid pace or adjusted to fit into a seminar format. The discussion questions are designed to give you ideas on how to share your faith, and the appendix provides real, thought-provoking stories to inspire you as you begin your own journey of joining God on mission and sharing the Gospel with a hurting world in desperate need of Him.

An online class for Taking Back the Gospel is also in the works, and will be offered for both individuals and small groups. Check nancy-golden.com frequently for updates.

ACKNOWLEDGMENTS

While writing is a solitary endeavor, creating a book is done in community. Once the content has been written, an editor is hired to ensure the manuscript is polished, along with a graphic artist to create the book cover. Research for gaining the various permissions needed may mean reaching out to a variety of sources. Beta readers provide invaluable insights.

I am blessed with a wonderful husband – he takes on so many responsibilities to make it possible for me to devote the time I do to writing. His encouragement keeps me going when the trek gets hard. Thank you, Phil – I love you, and I couldn't do it without you. I am so grateful we are traveling this road together!

I deeply appreciate all of the members of our family and the constant support they offer. The journey is so much sweeter when it is shared with them. Sister Janet Parker, brother Eddie Venetucci, sisters-in-law Jane Vaughan and Susan Venetucci, son Joshua Golden, and daughter-in-law Naomi Golden, thank you for always being my cheerleaders!

I want to thank my creative partners in this endeavor. My editor, Joseph Fredrickson, has once again helped me finalize my manuscript so that I can be confident I am giving my readers the experience they deserve. I am grateful Betty Martinez returned to help me refine my vision for the cover. Much appreciation to Thandinkosi, for helping smooth my author journey. Robyn Flach has been a tireless advocate in the difficult area of book promotion and her artistic flair has helped bring Taking Back Lent to the world.

I also want to give special thanks to Ross Irvin. Besides being a wonderful friend and encourager, he is also a gifted author. If it weren't for Ross, this book wouldn't exist. The idea for Taking Back Lent came from a comment Ross made after reading my Christmas Devotional, Taking Back Advent: Moving from the Mundane to the Miraculous. He asked me when I was going to write my next "Taking Back" book, and from his question, Taking Back Lent was born.

My dear friend Mary Oller is such a blessing! Thank you for your continual support, and most of all, for your love.

I am so thankful for the writing gifts God has blessed me with and that perhaps He is using my writing to draw people to Him and to renew/strengthen their faith. How wonderful it is that God will use us to further His kingdom! Ephesians 3:20-21 come to mind:

Now to him who is able to do immeasurably more than all we ask or imagine, according to his power that is at work within us, to him be glory in the church and in Christ Jesus throughout all generations, for ever and ever! Amen.

POSTSCRIPT

While I found it challenging to write so many devotionals, I truly enjoyed the process, and I hope my efforts bless you. If it does, please recommend Taking Back Lent to your family and friends.

Being an author is hard work, but it's also a joy. My heart's desire is for the words I write to have a positive impact on you. If you enjoyed this devotional, I would love to hear from you. You can email me directly with your comments at nancy@ goldencrossranch.com

One of the very best things you can do for an author is to leave a review on Amazon and/or Goodreads – I hope you'll consider doing so.

May the grace and peace of our Lord Jesus Christ be with you always,

Nancy Golden

ABOUT THE AUTHOR

Nancy Golden graduated from Dallas Christian College and earned her master's degree (MAR) from Liberty Baptist Theological Seminary. She is an adjunct faculty member at Dallas Christian College and an instructor for BeADisciple.com.

Nancy's seminary work includes Theology, Bible, and Intercultural Studies in Religion. Nancy and her husband, Phil, are members of Living Word Global Church in Irving, Texas. Nancy is an avid horsewoman and loves to sing praise and worship songs when she is riding.

Nancy writes across several genres with a focus on entertaining, clean, uplifting fiction and non-fiction. Visit Nancy's author website at https://nancy-golden.com to learn more about her writing projects and read her ramblings about this journey called life.

ALSO BY NANCY GOLDEN

Taking Back Advent

Alien Neighbors

Sword of Fate